International Finance
for
Food Security

A WORLD BANK PUBLICATION

International Finance for Food Security

Barbara Huddleston
D. Gale Johnson
Shlomo Reutlinger
Alberto Valdés

Published for The World Bank
The Johns Hopkins University Press
Baltimore and London

The Johns Hopkins University Press
Baltimore, Maryland 21218, U.S.A.

The views and interpretations in this book are the authors' and should not be attributed to the World Bank, to its affiliated organizations, or to any individual acting on their behalf.

First printing April 1984

EDITOR Virginia deHaven Hitchcock
FIGURES Pensri Kimpitak
COVER DESIGN Joyce C. Eisen

Library of Congress Cataloging in Publication Data

Main entry under title:

International finance for food security.

Bibliography: p.
Includes index.
1. Food Supply—Developing countries—Finance—International cooperation. I. Huddleston, Barbara, 1939- . II. World Bank.
HD9018.D44I57 1984 338.1'81 83-48109
ISBN 0-8018-3070-2

Contents

FIGURES

TABLES

Preface

THIS STUDY WAS CONCEIVED as a follow-up to research on the costs and benefits of an insurance scheme to provide food security for developing countries. A food financing facility would provide funds to a developing country to help it pay for cereal imports in years when costs are relatively high because of poor crops or high international market prices.

The study's objective was to consider the merits and probable effect of alternative designs for a food financing facility and to assess the one finally adopted by the International Monetary Fund (IMF) in May 1981. The work was carried out in three stages. First, each of the authors conducted preliminary data analyses and informal interviews with responsible officials in six sample countries expected to benefit from creation of a food financing facility. Second, a simulation model was constructed to analyze the effect of different methods of providing financial insurance against high food import bills in the sample countries. The effects were analyzed under three sets of assumptions about the countries' domestic food policies. Third, a price-forming equation for wheat was derived and used to test the likely effect of the financial facility in world markets under different conditions of supply and stocks.

The results support the decision of the IMF to integrate a food financing facility with its previously existing compensatory financing facility for export earnings, but they show that the degree to which individual countries will benefit depends greatly on their domestic food policies. The facility is expected to have negligible effect on world markets, except in years when the ratio of cereal stocks to anticipated demand is low and drawings from the facility are high. However, individual countries could significantly improve their food security position by using the facility to offset adverse local conditions, even when the world situation is normal.

The study was carried out with funding from the Rockefeller Foundation, and the support is gratefully acknowledged. The study seeks to shed light on issues that are pertinent for policy discussion and to contribute to the debate on the merits of the facility. World Bank publishes works that seek to draw out the policy significance of a particular topic, as this study tries to do for the financial facility. With the Rockefeller Foundation, the Bank is a co-funder of the Consultative Group in International Agricultural Research, to which the International Food Policy Research Institute (IFPRI) belongs. The Bank, the Foundation, and the authors therefore agreed that the Bank could properly publish a study that represented a joint effort by one of its staff, two IFPRI staff, and a project leader selected by the Foundation.

D. Gale Johnson, professor at the University of Chicago, served as project leader; Shlomo Reutlinger, research economist at the World Bank, developed the country impact simulation model; and Barbara Huddleston and Alberto Valdés, research fellows at IFPRI, prepared the price analysis. All shared equally in preparing the final report. The views expressed are those of the authors and not those of any of the institutions with which they are affiliated, nor of the Rockefeller Foundation. The authors gratefully acknowledge the assistance of S. Yalamanchili with the simulation model and of Stephen Haykin for the price-forming equation.

International Finance
for
Food Security

1
Introduction and Summary

NATIONAL FOOD POLICIES in developing countries are increasingly influenced by global events and international policies beyond the control of individual governments. During the 1960s and 1970s developing countries stepped up their imports of food substantially, and thus their food supply policies have become more dependent on imports. For some countries the variability in food supplies and consumption presents a serious problem. A country experiences food insecurity when no measures are taken to cushion the effects of production and price variations on consumption. Conversely, food security is the assurance that supplies and financing will be available to meet minimally adequate consumption requirements without domestic price increases, regardless of world market conditions.

The main causes of food insecurity in developing countries are fluctuations in domestic production and in the price of imported cereals. Taken together, the level of domestic production and the level of imports determine the supply available to meet consumer demand. When supplies are short, domestic prices rise, and people respond by reducing the amount they consume. Although part of the variability in food production is counteracted by changes in stocks held by farmers, consumers, and marketing agencies as well as in net trade flows, some instability in food supply remains. This instability will be aggravated if increases in the world price of cereals prevent countries from importing additional quantities to offset domestic shortages. The

Table 1. *Variability in the Consumption of Staple Foods, 1961 to 1976*

Region and country	Instability in consumption of staple foods: Standard deviation[a] (thousands of metric tons)	Instability in consumption of staple foods: Coefficient of variation (percent)	Probability of actual consumption falling below 95 percent of trend
Asia			
Bangladesh	1,013	7.6	26
India	5,570	5.3	17
Indonesia	1,204	6.1	21
Korea, Republic of	531	6.5	22
Philippines	192	3.3	6
Sri Lanka	163	8.3	27
North Africa/Middle East			
Algeria	667	24.6	42
Egypt	1,164	12.6	34
Jordan	88	21.2	40
Libya	115	16.7	38
Morocco	933	19.3	40
Syria	360	18.7	39
Sub-Saharan Africa			
Ghana	134	6.1	21
Nigeria	965	5.6	19
Senegal	319	15.7	37
Tanzania	517	14.6	37
Upper Volta	126	9.5	30
Zaire	172	4.1	11
Latin America			
Brazil	1,955	5.8	20
Chile	386	14.4	36
Colombia	147	4.7	14
Guatemala	69	6.9	24
Mexico	757	5.3	17
Peru	110	3.9	10

a. Defined as the standard deviation of the consumption variable $C_t - \hat{C}_t$.

Source: Alberto Valdés and Panos Konandreas, "Assessing Food Insecurity Based on National Aggregates in Developing Countries," in Alberto Valdés, ed., *Food Security for Developing Countries* (Boulder, Col.: Westview Press, 1981), p. 30.

country's balance of payments position may also have an effect on food security if additional demand for foreign exchange for food imports coincides with reduced export earnings.

The effect of fluctuations in domestic production on producer incomes is another cause of food insecurity. A poor harvest reduces the ability of rural people to purchase food and causes prices to rise when reductions in domestic output are not offset by other sources of supply. Relatively minor shortfalls in the incomes of small farmers resulting from production shortfalls often considerably reduce food consumption. The bulk of the adjustment to smaller food supplies falls on the poor, whose consumption levels already are low. For them, a drop in consumption results in energy-deficient diets, with long-run consequences for health and productivity.

Unstable levels of food consumption in developing countries have received much attention in recent years. Although there are no precise measures of annual changes in per capita food consumption, the available data, summarized in Table 1, indicate a large degree of variability in several developing countries. For example, the last column shows that in Algeria and Morocco per capita food consumption may be 5 percent or more below trend in two years out of five. In India and Nigeria staple food consumption will fall 5 percent or more below trend in one year out of five. Variable consumption is the direct consequence of variability in consumers' incomes and of food prices. Thus, the extent to which variable domestic production and world prices result in variable consumption depends very much on the domestic policies that a country pursues.

In the past, the most frequently advocated remedy for increasing food security was to build up large buffer stocks, both on an international scale and in each of the countries with highly variable production. On closer examination, however, the buffer stock option has not proved cost effective or realistic for most countries. The developed countries did not wish to underwrite the high costs of international stocks that would be large enough to stabilize global supplies and the international price of grains. In any case, they could not agree on a mutually satisfactory formula for sharing costs. National stocks large enough to stabilize domestic supplies in each developing country against fluctuations in domestic harvests and foreign exchange availability would have required huge investments, which these countries could ill afford to make.

To effectively counter fluctuations in consumption among the rural population, countries need to do much more than stabilize the national supply and price of food. When incomes are depressed because of a poor harvest, special programs are also needed to maintain incomes, such as assured credit and public employment and procurement at prices that compensate for the reduced volume of sales. When it is not feasible to stabilize incomes, food should be distributed at subsidized prices. Another essential instrument for assuring food security is a well-functioning internal trade sector which minimizes price differences among regions within countries. Thus, on-farm and regional stocks, low-cost transport, a smooth flow of information, and a trading sector that responds quickly to imbalances in supply are also essential to food security.

Freer trade could contribute significantly to stabilizing international prices. If international trade in agricultural products had been free in the 1970s, price variability in international markets would have been sharply reduced. But neither the industrial nor the developing countries are ready to significantly reduce barriers to trade in food products. Consequently, increased food security must be attained by other means.

A developing country now can stabilize its food supply in several ways. One is to reduce fluctuations in domestic food production, primarily by increasing irrigation. A second is to build up stocks in years of high production for use during poor years. Both of these options involve a substantial commitment of resources. An alternative is to vary the volume of food imports inversely with changes in domestic production.[1] Under existing institutional arrangements, however, developing countries may not have sufficient foreign exchange resources to use this option. A food financing facility would minimize this constraint.

The Financial Facility Concept

The financial remedy examined and advocated in this monograph grows out of a realization that the malady is not so much the international instability in food supplies, but the inability of the poorest and most financially strained countries to secure a minimally adequate food supply. A food financing facility provides the means for such countries to maintain or increase imports when domestic supply is inadequate.

The concept of a foreign exchange constraint has meaning for food imports and food security because it is assumed that the exchange rate is not and should not be adjusted to offset a short-run unexpected increase in the food import bill. Furthermore, since low-income countries often cannot borrow on short notice in international capital markets at average lending rates when food import bills are abnormally high, international financial arrangements are needed to avoid reductions in consumption. Many countries, particularly middle-income developing countries, can draw on foreign currency reserves in years when their aggregate import bill increases sharply. For the poorest developing countries, with low reserve ratios, however, the flexibility to use reserve holdings is, naturally, limited.

Of course, a scheme to cover the excess cost of cereal imports can stabilize consumption for low-income families only if their purchasing power is maintained. A financial facility to reduce

1. D. Bigman and Shlomo Reutlinger, "Food Price Stabilization: National Buffer Stocks and Trade Policies," *American Journal of Agricultural Economics*, vol. 61, no. 4 (November 1979).

constraints on food imports is by no means the only thing necessary to achieve food security. Fluctuations in consumption will persist unless incomes and food prices are stabilized. Income stabilization requires such measures as public works, crop insurance, an adequate supply of credit, and publicly sponsored food distribution schemes. Price stabilization is promoted by improved transport and communication, which facilitate trading within a country and the imposition of subsidies for imports when world prices rise or of taxes when they fall. Yet even where policies to stabilize consumption are still rudimentary, deteriorating nutritional status in urban and rural areas can be alleviated if the country can import enough food to maintain stable domestic prices, regardless of fluctuations in domestic production or world markets. It is primarily in this context that international arrangements specifically designed to facilitate adequate food imports are being advocated. More cost effective than buffer stocks, a reliable financial facility enables countries to invest more of their scarce capital in agricultural and general development, and less in the construction of storage buildings and the maintenance of large grain inventories.

A Simulation Model

This study uses a simulation model to analyze the probable benefits and the pursuant demands on an internationally sponsored scheme for insuring against high food import bills. In this model, the instability of food consumption has been assumed to result primarily from variations in the domestic price of food. These prices are assumed to fluctuate either because the world price fluctuates or because the domestic supply plus imports differs from the amount that people will consume at the prevailing world price. In both cases, government policies and balance of payment constraints play an important role. To insulate the domestic price from world market prices, governments must subsidize domestic food prices or tax imports. To permit enough imports to satisfy demand at the world market price, there must be unrestricted allocations of foreign exchange.

The model allows for random fluctuations in the domestic harvest, the world price, and availability of foreign exchange. The incidence of food insecurity (that is, the probability of food consumption falling below a specified level) is estimated under different specifications of government policy affecting the insulation of domestic price from the world price and the allocation of foreign exchange to food and nonfood imports. It is also estimated for different possible schemes for reducing foreign exchange constraints.

Three possible schemes to reduce foreign exchange constraints have been specified: compensation for shortfalls in foreign exchange earnings (similar to the original compensatory financing facility, CFF, of the International Monetary Fund, IMF); compensation for excessive food import bills; and compensation for any shortfalls in foreign exchange arising because the algebraic sum of export earnings and food import bills is less than normal (approximating the expanded CFF recently created in the IMF). For each financial scheme the model also estimates the amount of funds that would be withdrawn from a financial facility and the additional amount of imports that would be necessary.

The simulation experiments for six sample countries illustrate the strong influence of a government's policies on its food security and on its likely drawings from an international financing facility. Differences in food security among countries are caused more by different policies pursued by their governments than by differences in the stability of food production and the availability of foreign exchange.

The simulation experiments further illustrate that food security will be increased if countries have access to an integrated CFF, whether or not countries pursue policies to increase their food security. If a country does not insulate its internal food price from fluctuations in the international price and gives low priority to food imports, however, food insecurity will persist despite access to a financial facility. The gains in food security will be most pronounced if the existence of the financial facility encourages countries to adopt policies to increase their food security.

For the six sample countries, the expansion of a facility from one that compensates only for shortfalls in foreign exchange earnings to one that compensates for the algebraic sum of shortfalls arising from variations in foreign exchange earnings and food import bills implies an approximate doubling of expected annual drawings. Both the gains in food security and the expected drawings were calculated on the assumption that drawings are not constrained by a quota. Without quota limits the expansion of the CFF is expected to increase annual food imports from 20 to 45 percent of current levels. The smaller gain applies if countries were already pursuing policies to increase their food security before a financial facility was introduced. In this case, drawings from the facility are to a larger extent used to reduce the disruption in nonfood imports caused by these policies.

The simulation experiments yielded a set of predicted changes in food security that would result from new financial arrangements. Since the results are sensitive to the domestic food policies of the individual governments, the predictions are only conditional. They must be supplemented with speculations about the prevailing policies with and without a financial facility in the respective countries. In any case, the simulations anticipate the possible consequences of the financial facility and suggest complementary steps to achieve food security.

The IMF Facility

In May 1981 the IMF created an integrated financial facility for food imports by amending its CFF for export earnings to cover excess cereal import bills. Under the old rules the facility provided foreign exchange credit to cover shortfalls from trend in export earnings. Under the new rules, the shortfall in net export earnings would be calculated as trend exports minus actual exports plus actual cereal import costs minus trend cereal import costs. Credit would then be provided to cover the shortfall in net export earnings. The total amount of the drawing is constrained to 100 percent of quota for each of the two components and 125 percent of quota for the combined total. Countries can choose whether to draw under the new or the old rules, depending on which seem more beneficial. Once having chosen, a country cannot select the other option for three years. Repayment at below market rates is required within three to five years after the initial drawing.

A second proposal for creating a separate food financing facility within the IMF was rejected by the Fund's board. Under this proposal, the new facility would have provided credit equal to the excess of current cereal import bills over their trend value.

This study indicates that the integrated facility as adopted is preferable to a separate facility with comparable quota limits. The integrated scheme would result in lower average drawings for food imports than a separate facility because high food import bills are sometimes offset by high export earnings. However, the integrated scheme allows for substantially larger drawings in years when cereal production is short, cereal import prices are high, and foreign exchange is not readily available. In such years, the integrated scheme would supply most of the required foreign exchange, providing that quota limits are not unduly restricting. This arrangement could provide food security to developing countries when they most need it, but could still keep operating costs reasonable.

The financial facility adopted by the IMF will provide assistance only when import bills are above normal for reasons beyond control of the governments requesting help. Benefits will not be available to maintain or increase per capita consumption when government policies and economic trends lead to declines in the country's normal degree of self-sufficiency. A financial facility would help create conditions that favor food security. To realize these advantages, however, many countries would need to stabilize food consumption and prices. Because of the difficulties in achieving these objectives, use of the facility will probably grow slowly.

The facility will complement existing food aid, which is likely to decrease in volume when cereal prices rise. Food financing is less subject to political criteria than food aid. An international agreement on holding grain reserves would not be required. Undoubtedly, larger grain reserves could reduce the variations in world price, but the tangible effects of the agreement envisioned under the Wheat Trade Convention are questionable.[2]

This analysis indicates that world price reacts to reductions in world stock levels only when the initial level is relatively low compared with estimated world demand. As the ratio of stocks to demand falls below about 17 to 20 percent, prices start to increase at a faster rate. During the 1970s world stocks declined relative to world consumption. Depending on the production policies of major exporters and the consumption policies of centrally planned importers, stocks may not increase relative to consumption for the foreseeable future. If this is so, greater variations in world prices can be expected.

The IMF food facility will not prevent international price increases caused by emergencies. If such price increases occur, however, the facility should ease the strain for cereal-importing countries whose costs suddenly rise sharply. Even when cereals are in short supply worldwide, the increase in imports financed by a facility would be small relative to the volume of international trade. At such times, however, the ratio of world stocks to demand will probably be low, and the shock of an additional 10

2. Daniel T. Morrow, *The Economics of the International Stockholding of Wheat*, Research Report no. 18 (Washington, D.C.: International Food Policy Research Institute, 1980).

to 20 million tons of demand at such times could affect prices noticeably. In most years neither the size of stocks nor the shift in demand are likely to be extreme, and the effect on world price would be small. For individual countries receiving assistance, however, the additional imports might be significant and could mean the difference between adequate consumption or deprivation for many poor people in the developing world.

2
Sources of Food Insecurity

DURING THE TWO DECADES that ended in 1972 low-income countries whose food production varied significantly from year to year could be assured that grain would be available at prices that changed little from year to year. For example, between 1960 and 1971 the largest year-to-year percentage change in U.S. export prices of corn and wheat was 16 percent. The highest annual average export price for wheat was US$67 per metric ton in 1966, and the lowest was US$53 in 1969. For corn, the range was from US$61 in 1971, when the corn blight reduced U.S. production, to US$47 in 1960. World market prices were stable even during the early and mid-1960s when world grain production was significantly below normal. Except for 1951 and 1952, during the Korean War, world market prices for grains also were stable during the 1950s.

Increased Variability of International Grain Prices

The situation has changed significantly since 1971 as international grain prices have become highly variable. The U.S. export price of wheat more than doubled in current dollars between 1972 and 1974 and then declined 71 percent by 1977 (more than 50 percent in constant dollars). Between August 1977 and August 1979 the export price of wheat again increased 80 percent. For corn, the price rose more than 130 percent between 1972 and 1974, and then declined. During the calendar year

1980 corn export prices increased by almost 50 percent, primarily in response to a reduced U.S. corn crop and a second year of low yields in the Soviet Union. In addition, variability in ocean shipping rates also appears to have increased, although significantly less than that of grain prices.

The coefficients of variation shown in Figure 1 dramatize the increased variability of export prices for wheat and rice. During the 1970s wheat prices varied more than eight times as much as during the 1960s. For rice, the export price variability more than doubled.

Figure 1. *Variability in Real Export Prices for Wheat and Rice, 1950 to 1979*

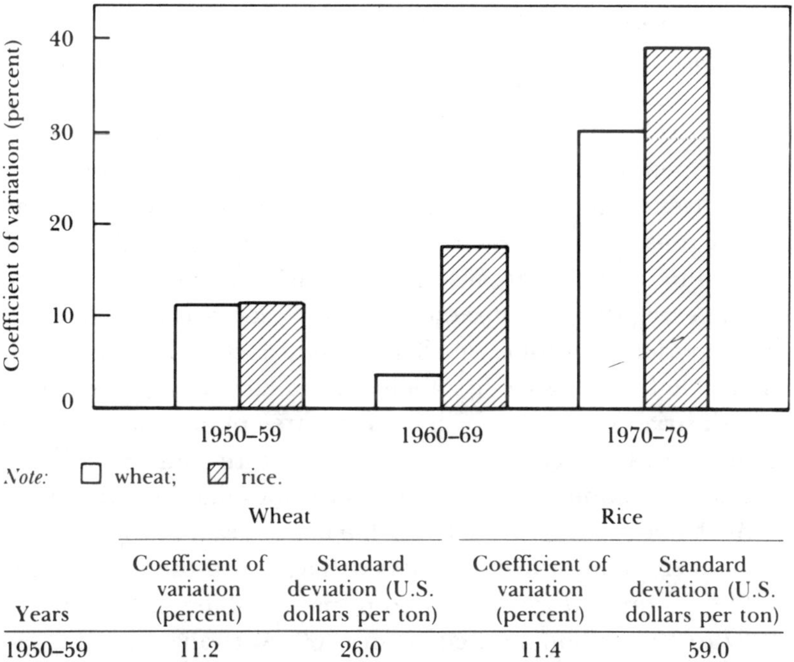

Note: ☐ wheat; ▨ rice.

	Wheat		Rice	
Years	Coefficient of variation (percent)	Standard deviation (U.S. dollars per ton)	Coefficient of variation (percent)	Standard deviation (U.S. dollars per ton)
1950–59	11.2	26.0	11.4	59.0
1960–69	3.6	7.0	17.5	89.0
1970–79	30.0	56.0	39.0	187.6

Source: World Bank data.

International Price Stability up to the Mid-1970s

The major reasons grain prices were stable during 1952–72 were the support policies of the United States and Canada. Very large quantities of grain were either owned or controlled by the two governments. In addition, the major exporters could produce more grain than was demanded at politically acceptable prices. The tendency for stocks to grow was somewhat abated by efforts to limit output, especially in the United States, and by extensive use of food aid. Price stability was not the objective of these farm price policies, but was instead a consequence of agricultural price and income policies designed to bring grain production into better balance with demand. This goal was largely achieved by the early 1970s, although it was perhaps not fully appreciated at the time.

Prices were stable during the 1960s despite unusually unstable grain production throughout the world. Shortfalls in grain production below normal during 1961/62–1965/66 exceeded those for 1970/71–1974/75 in absolute and relative terms. In the earlier period the algebraic sum of the departures above and below trend was 72 million metric tons compared with 62 million metric tons in 1970/71–1974/75. The relative shortfall also was greater in the 1960s because grain production grew by one third in the early 1970s. Consequently, the year-to-year fluctuations have gradually become smaller. Several factors have been responsible for this greater stability in production: mechanization in industrial countries, which has permitted more timely farming operations; summer fallow and other moisture-conserving methods of cultivation; and improved herbicides and insecticides.

By the beginning of the 1970s the major grain exporters were no longer willing to carry stocks as large as those of the early 1960s. As grain stocks increased from 70 million metric tons in 1967 to 105 million metric tons in 1969, Australia, Canada, and the United States made major efforts to reduce the production of wheat through programs to limit output or acreage. Before 1970 neither Canada nor Australia had made significant efforts to limit wheat production. Wheat and feed grain stocks held by the major exporters in 1961/62 were 14.4 percent of world production, compared with 9.6 percent in 1970/71 and 8.6 percent in 1972/73.

International Price Instability since the Mid-1970s

A change in U.S. grain storage policies in the 1977 farm legislation will contribute to increasingly variable prices in the years ahead. The change reflected the belief that setting price supports near market prices had forced the United States to carry a large share of the world's grain stocks and, at the same time, to become a residual supplier in export markets. This was believed to have resulted in larger-than-desired expenditures for storage and supply management. In addition, farmers concluded that U.S. storage policies that led to stable prices also meant low prices. The 1977 U.S. farm legislation may have been the first in modern times that was deliberately designed to increase price instability.

The farmer-held grain reserve created by the 1977 act substantially increased the spread between the loan or support level and the prices at which grain either could be or would be removed from U.S. reserve stocks.[1] The Commodity Credit Corporation, which previously owned or controlled most grain stocks, was prohibited from selling any of its grain at less than 150 percent of the support price as long as there was any grain in the farmer-held reserve. And once grain was put into the farmer-held reserve, the government could not call the loans until the market prices were 40 percent above the support price for coarse grains and 75 percent above it for wheat. Thus the range of price variability provided for in the reserve program is

1. The term "farmer-held reserve" refers to stocks of grain owned by farmers but obligated to the government as collateral for price support loans. Previously, the government took possession of such grain when loans came due. Now, farmers retain the grain and receive a storage subsidy from the government. In exchange, they agree not to sell the grain until prices reach a prescribed level.

substantially greater than that of the 1950s and 1960s. Some proposals call for widening the price ranges further. No other major grain exporter has been willing to increase its stocks to offset the lower U.S. level, and there is no particular reason to expect any to do so.

National policies to stabilize domestic prices of grains and other agricultural products also have increased price instability in international grain markets. Except for Canada, Australia, the United States, and, in recent years, India, governments have not been willing to hold sufficient stocks to offset variations in domestic supply and demand. Instead, governments have sought to achieve price stabilization by varying net trade. Thus, the internal instability of these nations has been reflected in the international market and in the economies of countries that permit their domestic prices to vary with the international prices.

During the 1960s and 1970s an increasing share of the world's grain was produced and consumed in nations that achieved internal price stability through managed trade. Basic agricultural policies changed little, but the ability and the will to pursue more effective domestic price stabilization policies increased. For example, the basic features of the price policies for food and agriculture in the Soviet Union were essentially the same in 1972 as in 1963. Prices paid to producers, prices of farm inputs, and consumer prices were fixed. In 1972, however, there was a much greater effort to establish internal prices at levels that more nearly equated supply to demand. In the earlier period substantial shortfalls of supply relative to demand were tolerated; but in the later period serious efforts were made to eliminate or minimize them. Thus both the mean level and the year-to-year variations in net grain trade became much greater during the 1970s than during the 1960s.

Similar changes in price stabilization policies occurred in the European Economic Community (EEC). In addition, an increasing number of developing countries have either instituted price stabilization policies or made existing programs more effective.

There is no reason to expect that the international price instability caused by various national policies will diminish during the 1980s. If anything, it is likely to increase. Nor is there any reason to anticipate that the storage policies of the major grain exporters will change in such a way as to increase stock levels. There now appears to be a rough balance between supply and demand for grains produced by the four major grain exporters—the United States, Canada, Australia, and France—at politically acceptable price levels. As long as this situation prevails, there is no compelling reason for the major grain exporters to bear the costs of larger grain stocks.[2]

The increased price instability in international grain markets will cause greater variability in the grain and food import bills of the developing countries. In contrast to the 1960s, when food import bills varied primarily because of quantity changes, variation since then has been caused by both quantity and price.

Fluctuations in Domestic Food Production

Food production varies greatly for some individual countries but relatively little at the global level. This is the case for certain developed countries, such as the Soviet Union, as well as for many developing countries. Table 2 indicates that in ten of the twenty-four countries analyzed, production fell below 95 percent of trend approximately once every three years. Production has been more stable in large countries, such as India, Indonesia, Brazil, Bangladesh, and in those where a significant portion of cropland is irrigated, such as Egypt. The coefficient of variation for production in these countries is about 6 percent. In contrast, in several Arab countries the coefficient of variation is about 20

2. D. Gale Johnson, "The World Food Situation: Developments during the 1970s and Prospects for the 1980s," in *AEI Studies on Contemporary Economic Problems* (Washington, D.C.: American Enterprise Institute, 1980).

Table 2. *Variability in the Production of Staple Foods, 1961 to 1976*

Region and country	*Instability in production of staple foods:* *Standard deviation*[a] *(thousands of metric tons)*	*Coefficient of variation (percent)*[b]	*Probability of actual production falling below 95 percent of trend*
Asia			
Bangladesh	765	6.4	22
India	6,653	6.4	22
Indonesia	1,040	5.4	18
Korea, Republic of	445	7.1	24
Philippines	346	5.7	19
Sri Lanka	107	9.3	29
North Africa/Middle East			
Algeria	531	28.9	43
Egypt	282	4.5	13
Jordan	119	65.6	47
Libya	56	28.0	43
Morocco	1,156	27.2	43
Syria	702	38.8	45
Sub-Saharan Africa			
Ghana	121	5.8	20
Nigeria	958	5.7	19
Senegal	325	18.6	39
Tanzania	430	12.7	36
Upper Volta	128	9.8	30
Zaire	190	4.9	15
Latin America			
Brazil	1,631	5.2	17
Chile	215	11.1	33
Colombia	126	4.4	13
Guatemala	56	6.5	22
Mexico	1,060	7.7	26
Peru	197	9.8	30

a. Defined as the standard deviation of the production variable $Q_t - \hat{Q}_t$.

b. Defined as the standard deviation of the variable $(Q_t - \hat{Q}_t)/Q_t \cdot 100$.

Source: Alberto Valdés and Panos Konandreas, "Assessing Food Insecurity Based on National Aggregates in Developing Countries," in Alberto Valdés, ed., *Food Security for Developing Countries* (Boulder, Col.: Westview Press, 1981).

percent. Similarly, it is high in several sub-Saharan African countries, such as Senegal and Tanzania. The variability in the production of staple foods in ten selected countries is shown in Figure 2.

The historical record is unequivocal as to the effect of unstable cereal production on food consumption. As shown in Table 3, changes in the production of cereals are highly correlated with changes in total staple production in almost every country, although the proportion of cereals to other staples varies by country.

Cereal imports generally have been too small to compensate for shortfalls in production. Consequently, variability in consumption of cereals is highly correlated with changes in food production (see Table 3). Table 4 provides data on the level of the shortfalls that are made up each year by commercial imports

Figure 2. *Variability in the Production of Staple Foods, for Selected Countries, 1961 to 1976*

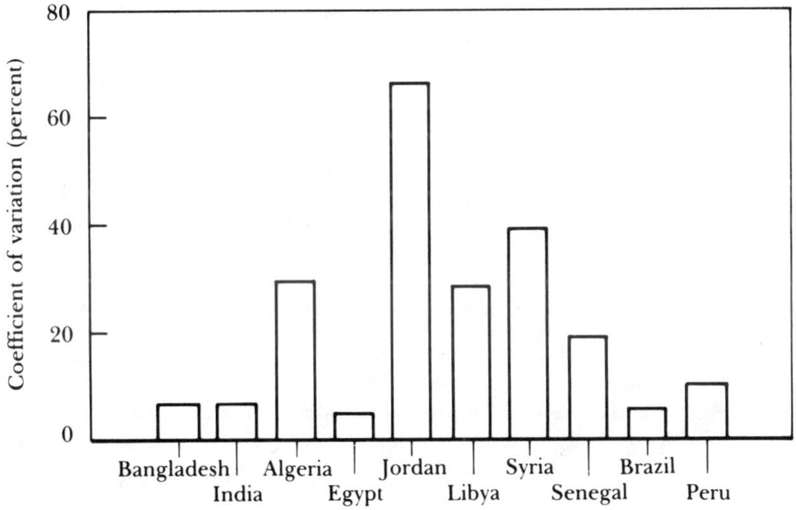

Table 3. *Correlation between Cereal and Total Staple Food Production and between Staple Food Production and Consumption, 1961 to 1976*

Region and country	*Correlation coefficient between cereal production and total staple food production*[a]	*Correlation coefficient between total staple food production and staple food consumption*[a]	*Correlation coefficient between export earnings and the food import bill*[b]
Asia			
Bangladesh	0.99	0.90	0.32
India	0.99	0.89	0.55
Indonesia	0.94	0.92	0.23
Korea, Republic of	0.96	0.20	0.21
Philippines	0.99	0.97	0.32
Sri Lanka	0.91	0.56	0.57
North Africa/Middle East			
Algeria	1.00	0.78	0.76
Egypt	0.96	0.29	0.49
Jordan	1.00	0.63	0.63
Libya	1.00	0.62	0.31
Morocco	0.96	0.98	0.32
Syria	1.00	0.92	0.13
Sub-Saharan Africa			
Ghana	0.93	0.98	0.38
Nigeria	0.92	0.99	−0.27
Senegal	0.81	0.99	−0.08
Tanzania	0.09	0.98	−0.65
Upper Volta	0.99	0.95	0.31
Zaire	−0.21	0.96	−0.15
Latin America			
Brazil	0.60	0.92	0.59
Chile	0.99	0.54	0.60
Colombia	0.85	0.51	−0.11
Guatemala	0.99	0.51	0.40
Mexico	1.00	0.53	0.15
Peru	0.97	0.37	−0.23

a. Staple food is defined as cereals, pulses, roots and tubers, and groundnuts.

b. Export earnings include goods and services.

Source: Alberto Valdés and Panos Konandreas, "Assessing Food Insecurity Based on National Aggregates in Developing Countries," in Alberto Valdés, ed., *Food Security for Developing Countries* (Boulder, Col.: Westview Press, 1981).

and food aid. Because of variations in production and stocks, this amount of imports exceeds requirements for some years, whereas in other years it is relatively low.

There are several possible reasons why consumption has been highly correlated with production in most of the countries studied: cereal production may be highly correlated with consumers' disposable income; cereal production may have a strong negative correlation with cereal import prices; market channels may not be flexible enough to handle large year-to-year changes in imported cereals; and, of course, foreign exchange allocations to food imports may have been overly restrictive. Because prices have been relatively stable for most of the period covered, negative correlation between production and import prices would not appear to be a significant factor.

Variability of Food Import Bills

Although changes in production are the main factors that induce variations in a country's food imports, the import bill is determined by both prices and quantities imported. During the 1960s, when prices were stable, variable import volumes were responsible for almost all of the variability in the cereal import bill for a sample of the developing countries (Table 5). In five of the eighteen countries, changes in import volume were responsible for at least 75 percent of the variability in the cereal import bill.

In contrast, during the 1970s, price changes were responsible for more than 50 percent of the total variability of the food import bill in ten out of the eighteen countries. Variability in import volume was still substantial and clearly dominant for several countries, such as Tanzania, Upper Volta, and Mali. In both periods, however, food import bills would have been much higher if countries had sought to obtain food security during

Table 4. *Role of Cereal Imports in Meeting Shortfalls in Domestic Cereal Production for the Greatest and Smallest Shortfalls, 1965 to 1977*

		Greatest shortfall		
Region and country	*Year*	*Level of shortfall (thousands of metric tons)*	*Commercial imports (thousands of metric tons)*	*Food aid (thousands of metric tons)*
Asia				
Bangladesh[b]	1971	3,536	1,164	n.a.
India	1965	17,820	1,063	6,814
Indonesia	1967	2,112	497	108
Philippines	1966	983	578	47
Sri Lanka	1975	1,121	977	188
North Africa/Middle East				
Egypt	1973	4,470	1,858	14
Jordan	1977	329	238	147
Somalia	1977	110	120	17
Syria	1971	1,009	794	8
Sub-Saharan Africa				
Mali	1972	136	30	40
Senegal	1977	338	405	15
Tanzania	1974	322	430	1
Upper Volta	1977	116	45	6
Latin America				
Bolivia	1977	284	230	9
Brazil	1966	3,490	2,088	365
Chile	1975	822	401	314
Haiti	1977	222	107	80
Peru	1975	811	1,130	13

Note: The shortfall is defined as the difference between constant consumption of cereal per capita (using a 1961–65 base) and the domestic supply of cereal. The supply includes available data on changes in stocks as well as in the levels of domestic cereal production. Data on stock changes may not always be reliable, as they are often imputed from other supply data rather than reported directly. Cereals include wheat, wheat flour (in wheat equivalents), rice, maize, rye, and cereals not elsewhere specified.

	Smallest shortfall			
Year	*Level of shortfall*[a] *(thousands of metric tons)*	*Commercial imports (thousands of metric tons)*	*Food aid (thousands of metric tons)*	*Number of years with uncompensated shortfall*
1973	1,871	1,921	935	5
1977	−9,997	30	939	2
1977	−1,605	1,874	924	2
1977	−475	838	30	1
1968	718	774	180	4
1968	1,551	2,416	1	4
1965	104	123	16	5
1972	17	53	15	4
1976	120	195	77	9
1965	5	22	0	7
1967	185	191	46	4
1966	−68	74	5	6
1968	−15	20	0	8
1965	148	68	99	7
1977	−4,414	2,644	5	1
1971	−73	475	13	4
1967	42	36	1	9
1967	430	547	7	4

n.a. Not available.

a. A negative shortfall indicates a surplus supply of domestic cereal over the constant level of cereal required per capita.

b. Includes 1971–77 data.

Source: Data compiled by Grant Scobie and Alberto Valdés, IFPRI.

Table 5. *Variability of the Cereal Import Bill, 1961 to 1978*
(percent)

Region and country	Cause of variability of import bill		
	1961–70		
	Volume	*Price*	*Interaction*
Asia			
Bangladesh	97.9	2.2	−16.3
India	98.7	1.3	−43.3
Indonesia	90.6	9.4	5.4
Philippines	78.2	21.8	108.3
Sri Lanka	91.4	8.6	−20.2
North Africa/Middle East			
Egypt	91.7	8.3	183.1
Jordan	92.0	8.0	31.8
Somalia	90.1	9.9	56.7
Syria	82.0	18.0	−58.2
Sub-Saharan Africa			
Mali	77.4	22.6	103.8
Senegal	42.5	57.5	58.4
Tanzania	93.3	6.7	16.6
Upper Volta	44.4	55.6	182.8
Latin America			
Bolivia	73.0	27.0	99.2
Brazil	86.2	13.8	358.6
Chile	90.6	9.4	−20.0
Haiti	84.9	15.1	118.1
Peru	78.6	21.4	94.6

Note: These figures are obtained by dividing the variance of the actual food import bill by the variance of the import volume (times the average price) and the variance of the import price (times the average volume of imports). The methodology is found in Valdés and Konandreas, "Assessing Food Insecurity." The quoted prices of imports used here represent their world prices and not

Cause of variability of import bill					
1970–78			*1961–78*		
Volume	*Price*	*Interaction*	*Volume*	*Price*	*Interaction*
52.7	47.3	−12.5	57.3	42.7	20.1
83.3	16.7	21.5	65.0	35.0	−21.3
41.7	58.3	−61.3	40.5	59.5	−52.0
34.8	65.2	−76.6	31.7	68.3	−59.4
13.0	87.0	−22.7	11.2	88.9	−36.1
35.4	64.6	3.3	25.8	74.2	22.8
41.3	58.7	−45.1	34.7	65.3	−41.6
39.6	60.4	−62.9	39.7	60.3	−45.1
52.3	47.7	−83.9	49.0	51.1	−75.2
84.6	15.5	96.9	82.6	17.4	263.1
20.7	79.3	−55.1	13.7	86.3	−57.3
76.3	23.7	117.7	74.9	25.1	229.6
59.1	40.9	−48.4	53.2	41.8	−16.6
14.1	85.9	−39.7	9.4	99.6	−50.7
51.4	48.6	−20.7	32.9	67.1	−16.2
57.2	42.8	60.9	47.3	52.7	118.2
36.8	63.2	−15.7	29.3	70.7	11.4
26.7	73.3	55.6	22.1	77.9	69.8

the true cost of the portion imported under food aid programs. It is assumed that import volumes including food aid can be treated as the minimum desired level that developing countries would have imported even without food aid.

Source: Data compiled by Grant Scobie and Alberto Valdés, IFPRI.

the period. In fact, preliminary calculations suggest average annual increases for 1965–76 of about US$0.2 to US$1.1 billion.[3]

An increase in world carryover stocks, presumably the objective of a new Wheat Trade Convention, could conceivably benefit developing countries by decreasing the variability of world prices of wheat. Nevertheless, even if the variation in world prices is reduced, the variation in a country's own levels of production must still be dealt with.

Food Import Bills and Foreign Exchange

The availability of foreign exchange could be the most critical factor in determining whether a country can import enough food to stabilize consumption. The average ratios of the food import bill to total export revenues (goods and services) presented in Table 6 for twenty-four developing countries indicate the pressure of food imports on their balances of trade. The ratios underestimate the pressure exerted by the food imports that would have been needed to stabilize consumption in 1965 to 1977 because these imports already had been affected by shortages of foreign exchange.

3. Alberto Valdés and Panos Konandreas, "Assessing Food Insecurity Based on National Aggregates in Developing Countries," in Alberto Valdés, ed., *Food Security for Developing Countries* (Boulder, Col.: Westview Press, 1981), table 2.8. Estimates of the actual increase in the net import bill depend on country coverage and assumptions about the responses of these countries to fluctuations in domestic production and world market price. The net increase in the import bill is defined as the increase in the import bill offset by any increase in export earnings during the period in question. Both estimates shown are calculated for sixty-seven developing countries (excluding eight major oil exporters). The lower estimate is calculated using historical import levels for these sixty-seven countries during this twelve-year period. The larger estimate is calculated assuming that the import levels of the countries would have stabilized consumption at levels consistent with the historical growth rate. This means that imports are adjusted upward for years when there is a shortfall in actual consumption, but are adjusted downward when actual consumption levels rise above trend levels.

A large food import bill could be small relative to a country's total export revenues, or vice versa. Similarly, the fluctuations of a country's food import bill may coincide with or diverge from fluctuations in its export earnings or with other important imports, such as petroleum products. The higher the food import bill relative to the supply of foreign exchange, or the lower the correlation between the food import bill and foreign exchange earnings, the more severe is the problem of food imports. In general, food import bills are positively correlated to export earnings in most countries. This implies that, for those countries, in years when the food import bill is higher, foreign exchange earnings are also higher.

The mean ratios in Table 6 for the normal years between 1965 and 1977 do not suggest a severe constraint for some countries, particularly in Latin America. But the high ratios for many low-income countries, notably Egypt, Sri Lanka, Bangladesh, and India, do. The fact that food aid is used by some countries to ease the constraint does not lessen the importance of the problem.

In years of higher import prices, domestic production shortfalls, or lower export revenues, the pressure of the food import bill on a country's overall import capacity was considerable. For some countries with low average ratios, such as Syria, the ratio increased by a factor of three or four in exceptionally unfavorable years. For several low-income countries, particularly in Asia and Africa, this ratio was intolerably high in some years. For a few developing countries, such as Nigeria, Libya, and Colombia, however, the ratio was remarkably low even at its maximum value.

The short-term implications of a large and unexpected increase in the food import bill can be portrayed in terms of the foreign exchange cost of the excess food import bill relative to the supply of foreign exchange.[4] Table 7 shows this for eighteen

4. Defined as $\{P_{it}(R_{it} - (QP_{it} - \Delta S_{it}) - M_{it})\}\ 1/F$, where P_{it} is the unit import

developing countries. For several of these countries the extra cost of cereal imports represented 10 percent and sometimes as much as 20 or 30 percent of the supply of foreign exchange. This was over and above the trend value of cereal imports in those years and represents unexpected short-run excess demand for foreign exchange.

A similar calculation for foreign exchange reserves showed that in some years the extra cost of cereal imports represented from 50 to 80 percent of the year's foreign exchange reserves (in India in 1975, Sri Lanka in 1973, and Haiti in 1977). In 1975 it even reached more than 100 percent for Tanzania, Sri Lanka, and Haiti. It remained a small fraction of reserves throughout the period for Peru, Chile, and the Philippines. Two qualifications are relevant here. First, as a proxy for import capacity more weight is given to the supply of foreign exchange than to reserves. A constant level of reserves is compatible with wide fluctuations in export earnings. Second, foreign exchange earnings, ideally, should be adjusted for changes in the nonfood import bill.

Thus, although all of the countries are food-deficit countries, the sample includes countries whose individual problems and prospects are far from identical. The flexibility of some of the countries in their use of reserve holdings has naturally been rather limited, particularly for the poorest developing countries whose reserve ratios have been low. Thus, the brunt of the adjustment is made in the allocation of foreign exchange among imports.

In many developing countries the problems created by the increase in the world price of cereals were compounded by the shortfalls in the domestic production of food. For some coun-

---

price in country i in year t; R_{it} represents requirements in metric tons of cereals in country i in year t reflecting annual population and income growth using FAO estimates of income elasticity of demand for cereals in 1975; QP_{it} and ΔS_{it} represent domestic production and changes in stocks, respectively; M_{it} represents a three-year moving average of cereal imports (both commercial imports and food aid); and F represents the supply of foreign exchange as defined in Table 7. All food imports are listed at commercial prices, including food aid.

Table 6. *Ratio of Food Imports to Total Export Revenues, 1965 to 1977*
(percent)

Region and country	*1965–67*	*1970–72*	*1975–77*	*1965–77 Mean*	*1965–77 Maximum*
Asia					
Bangladesh	n.a.	n.a.	67	77[a]	123 (1975)
India	40	10	24	23[b]	45 (1966)
Indonesia	7	13	6	11	21 (1968)
Korea, Republic of	13	16	7	13	22 (1969)
Philippines	7	5	4	5	9 (1965)
Sri Lanka	25	25	36	30	50 (1975)
North Africa/Middle East					
Algeria	8	6	9	7[c]	10 (1973)
Egypt	23	12	20	17	32 (1974)
Jordan	13	17	7	12[c]	18 (1972)
Libya	2	1	2	2[c]	3 (1975)
Morocco	9	6	2	8	14 (1975)
Syria	8	14	7	9	19 (1971)
Sub-Saharan Africa					
Ghana	5	3	4	4[c]	6 (1977)
Nigeria	3	2	2	2[c]	3 (1977)
Senegal	n.a.	10	10	10[d]	20 (1973)
Tanzania	3	3	10	6[c]	22 (1974)
Upper Volta	n.a.	8	9	9[e]	19 (1974)
Zaire	3	3	6	3[f]	6 (1975)
Latin America					
Brazil	10	4	4	6	11 (1967)
Chile	4	4	6	6	14 (1974)
Colombia	3	3	4	3	5 (1974)
Guatemala	3	2	3	3	4 (1975)
Mexico	1	2	5	3[c]	10 (1975)
Peru	6	5	11	7[c]	16 (1975)

Note: Export revenues include goods and services (except Brazil for 1965–67). The food import bill includes cereal and other staples. All food imports are listed at commercial prices, including food aid.

n.a. Not available.

a. 1973–77. c. 1967–77. e. 1968–75.
b. 1965–76. d. 1968–76. f. 1965–75.

Source: Ammar Siamwalla and Alberto Valdés, "Food Insecurity in Developing Countries," *Food Policy,* vol. 5, no. 4 (November 1980).

Table 7. *Foreign Exchange Cost of the Excess Food Import Bill, 1967 to 1977*
(percentage of the supply of foreign exchange)

Region and country	*1967*	*1969*	*1971*
Asia			
Bangladesh	n.a.	n.a.	n.a.
India	1.6	−7.5	2.4
Indonesia	28.7	8.7	11.3
Philippines	1.0	1.3	1.8
Sri Lanka	0.9	2.2	3.4
North Africa/Middle East			
Egypt	−3.8	2.4	1.7
Jordan	6.7	14.5	10.7
Somalia	6.5	0.7	−5.1
Syria	0.7	2.4	7.7
Sub-Saharan Africa			
Mali	7.5	−407.2	5.7
Senegal	n.a.	−2.2	1.9
Tanzania	9.6	10.9	6.1
Upper Volta	n.a.	7.5	7.4
Latin America			
Bolivia	1.7	3.9	2.8
Brazil	−0.8	6.8	7.0
Chile	−1.9	−0.2	−2.5
Haiti	1.3	4.3	3.6
Peru	−0.1	0.5	2.0

Note: The supply of foreign exchange includes total export receipts plus private unrequited transfers plus net capital inflow. Food includes cereals, meats, dairy products, fruits and vegetables, sugar, pulses, root crops, oilseeds and vegetable

tries, however, the increase in their food import bill coincided with an increase in their export earnings. In sixteen out of twenty-four countries during 1965–76, the absolute variability of the food import bill was smaller than the variability of export earnings. However, the opposite occurs in some large low-income countries (Bangladesh, India, and Sri Lanka). In general, food import bills were positively correlated with export revenues, reflecting positive correlations in world market price

1973	*1975*	*1977*	*Maximum value (1967–77)*
14.0	86.2	55.4	114.1 (1976)
−5.9	17.0	−1.3	17.0 (1975)
8.0	13.7	11.8	28.7 (1967)
3.0	1.7	0.9	3.4 (1974)
11.2	23.7	6.1	23.7 (1975)
4.2	−12.0	−5.3	4.2 (1973)
15.2	10.5	5.7	17.0 (1974)
−3.3	−1.5	−5.6	6.5 (1967)
10.7	5.3	5.1	12.7 (1968)
−9.9	−19.4	13.6	24.9 (1968)
0.0	1.6	0.7	3.2 (1968)
10.2	20.8	22.8	22.8 (1977)
5.1	7.0	13.5	14.5 (1976)
4.5	4.2	3.7	4.9 (1974)
10.4	12.2	5.0	12.4 (1974)
0.0	−1.9	−1.4	0.7 (1972)
7.8	17.5	11.7	17.5 (1975)
2.3	2.3	0.6	2.3 (1975)

oils, cocoa beans, and derivatives.

n.a. Not available.

Source: Data compiled by Grant Scobie and Alberto Valdés, IFPRI.

fluctuations.

There is not a one-to-one relation between the observed changes in the supply of foreign exchange and the actual imports of food. A reduction of *X* percent in export revenues will not necessarily lead to a reduction of *X* percent in food imports. Similarly, an increase of *X* percent in the supply of foreign exchange from export revenues or foreign borrowing is unlikely to increase food imports by the same percentage.

The observed instability in import volumes in developing countries is in itself some measure of success in domestic food security policies. Stabilizing trade is the right solution for most countries. But the indirect effects of import instability could be detrimental to productivity in the nonfood sector. The possibility of food imports crowding out the imports of essential raw materials and capital goods has been noted by several researchers, including Lofchie for Tanzania, Behrman for Chile, and Pitt for Indonesia.[5]

Grant Scobie has recently made a rigorous quantitative analysis of import demand for Egypt during the past twenty-five years. He observed that the decline in the volume of imports accompanying a fall in foreign exchange supplies has the greatest effect on industrial raw materials and capital goods, and he concludes that "the inelastic demand for food imports engendered by the food subsidy scheme is associated with fluctuations in output and investment in the industrial sector."[6]

Thus, in countries already committed to policies to stabilize food consumption, shocks in the current account could be absorbed primarily by adjusting nonfood imports. In other countries, however, the major adjustment could be in food imports. The adjustments will vary from one country to another, reflecting differences in food consumption policies, in the share of food imports in the current account, and in access to foreign borrowing.

5. M. F. Lofchie, "Agrarian Crisis and Economic Liberalization in Tanzania," *Journal of Modern African Studies*, vol. 16, no. 3 (1978), pp. 451–75; J. R. Behrman, *Foreign Trade Regimes and Economic Development: Chile*, Foreign Trade Regimes and Economic Development series, vol. 8 (New York: National Bureau of Economic Research, 1976); and M. M. Pitt, "Alternative Trade Strategies and Employment: Indonesia," in A. O. Krueger, H. B. Lary, T. Monson, and N. Akrasanee, eds., *Trade and Employment in Developing Countries*, vol. 1, Individual Studies (Chicago: University of Chicago Press, 1981), pp. 181–237.

6. Grant M. Scobie, *Food Subsidies: Their Impact on Foreign Exchange and Trade in Egypt*, Research Report no. 40 (Washington, D.C.: International Food Policy Research Institute, August 1983).

Adjustment to variability in food import bills also is affected by income. The greater ability of higher income countries to vary their level of imports of food lies to a large extent in their greater access to the international capital markets and in their foreign currency reserves. In contrast, low-income countries cannot borrow on short notice in international capital markets at average lending rates. Furthermore, the poorest developing countries, with low reserve ratios, have a limited ability to draw on reserve holdings. Thus, the brunt of the adjustment takes place in the allocation of foreign exchange among the various items, including food.

In summary, for many developing countries, particularly the poorest, the extra cost of food imports (net of changes in export revenues) has been significant in terms of losses in their real income and deficits in their trading accounts. Quantitative assessments of above-normal additions to the food import bill between 1965 and 1976, adjusting for changes in export revenues, indicate that this extra cost was particularly significant for low-income developing countries. If the countries had followed a policy to stabilize food consumption instead, the calculations indicate that the net increment in the import bill resulting from increased food imports (net of fluctuations in export revenues) would have been considerably higher.

To restore the balance in their current accounts, many developing countries have had to reduce the volume either of food imports or of other essential goods. Furthermore, the lack of responsiveness of food aid to widespread production shortfalls observed during the 1970s, which was aggravated in years of high world market prices such as in the early 1970s, clearly added to the burden of imports during years of sharp increases in the food import bill.[7]

7. Barbara Huddleston, "Responsiveness of Food Aid to Variable Import Requirements," in Alberto Valdés, ed., *Food Security for Developing Countries* (Boulder, Col.: Westview Press, 1981), pp. 287–306.

3
Alternative Financing Facilities

FLUCTUATIONS IN FOOD CONSUMPTION in developing countries are basically caused by variations in people's purchasing power and in the price of food. For the purpose of analyzing the effect of a food financing facility it is assumed that fluctuations in income are either of minor significance or that countries independently pursue policies to stabilize income.

In food importing countries food prices fluctuate either because world prices fluctuate or because imports are more or less than what people are willing to consume at the prevailing price. In both cases, government policies and balance of payment constraints play an important role. To insulate the domestic price from world market prices, governments must either subsidize or tax imports. Permitting all the imports that people are willing to consume at the world market price requires unrestricted allocations of foreign exchange.

At best, international financial assistance can alleviate the balance of payment constraints a government faces if it wants to institute policies to insulate food prices and if it wants to allocate enough foreign exchange to food imports to stabilize consumption. But the extent to which food security is actually achieved also depends significantly on each government's propensity to pursue policies that insulate the domestic food price from fluctuations in the world market price, and to actually allocate scarce foreign exchange to food rather than other imports.

The Simulation Model

A simple normative model can be constructed, based on plausible determining factors, to estimate a country's food consumption, including probability distributions of domestic food production, the price of imported food, the availability of foreign exchange, and the country's policies for insulating the domestic price from the world price and for allocating foreign exchange to food imports. A country's ability to maintain desired consumption is then simulated on the basis of 3,000 randomly drawn observations from these probability distributions, with and without a financial facility operating under various rules. The experiments were repeated with different sets of parameters reflecting different government policies, and the results were used to assess the effects of international assistance schemes. A detailed description of the model and of the data and parameters used in the analysis is provided in the Appendix.

The model describes a set of outcomes in relation to circumstances presumed to exist at present. The assessments of consumption stability can be extrapolated to future years to the extent that shifts in the demand and supply of food and the availability of foreign exchange occur at the same rate over time, to the extent that there is no perceptible upward or downward trend in the world price, and to the extent that the relative variance of the variables remains unchanged. Calls on a financial facility in this case would increase in proportion to the growth of consumption. Alternative assumptions concerning trends in domestic or international prices would, of course, change the outcomes.

The random variables affecting a country's aggregate food consumption in the model are domestic cereal production, world cereal availability, and the total domestic supply of foreign exchange. On the basis of a linear, kinked world demand function for cereals, a normal probability distribution of world cereal production is transformed into a skewed probability distribution of the cereal import price. Similarly, on the assumption that the desired level of nonfood imports is constant, the probability distribution of the total supply of foreign exchange is transformed into a probability distribution of foreign exchange available for food imports without having to reduce nonfood imports. The mean of this distribution is the food import bill, when actual domestic cereal production is equal to mean domestic cereal production and when the actual cereal import price is equal to the mean cereal import price.

Consumption stabilization in the model is determined by the extent to which desired consumption and desired imports are responsive to price and by the extent to which actual consumption and actual imports are reduced from desired levels when foreign exchange is scarce. Desired imports are the positive difference between desired consumption and food production. Desired consumption, according to the formulation presented here, has no normative connotations. To the extent that desired consumption is highly price responsive, it could be far below a level consistent with food security. Food security is measured by the likelihood of consumption falling below some prespecified level.

A scarcity of foreign exchange affecting food imports is assumed to prevail whenever the desired food import bill exceeds the amount of foreign exchange available for food imports without having to reduce nonfood imports. When this happens, foreign exchange will be apportioned according to the propensity to restrict foreign exchange allocations for food imports (m), and the related propensity to restrict foreign exchange allocations for nonfood imports ($1 - m$). The value of m can vary between zero and one. A country that accords high priority to food security will give first priority to food imports ($m = 0$), and actual food imports will always equal desired imports. At the other extreme ($m = 1$), the food import bill will not be allowed to exceed the supply of foreign exchange available for food imports when nonfood imports are at the desired level, and food imports will be restricted to the maximum amount that can be purchased given the available supply of foreign exchange for food, the price of the food to be imported, and the relevant exchange rate.

In the model, government policy can affect the stability of consumption either through internal price-stabilizing policies affecting the desired level of consumption, or through the propensity to restrict the amount of foreign exchange made available to food imports (m) when not enough foreign exchange is available to achieve the desired levels of both food and nonfood imports. The model indicates the extent of food security with and without price stabilization policies, and with high, medium, and low propensities to restrict food imports when foreign exchange is scarce (m = 1.0, 0.5, and 0.2, respectively). These propensities, as well as the implementation of internal stabilization policies, reflect governments' priorities and commitments to food security, but they also reflect uncontrollable constraints. Low-income countries and countries that even in normal years must devote a large share of their export earnings to food imports may not have the required financial reserves or access to capital markets and, thus, the flexibility to reduce nonfood imports such as oil.

The effect of different international financial assistance schemes operated in conjunction with a range of country policies is illustrated by reference to data reflecting instability and current levels of the world food price, production, imports, and foreign exchange availability in six countries: Bangladesh, India, Egypt, Senegal, Brazil, and Peru. The data and parameters used are approximations and thus only illustrate the range of outcomes from instituting different schemes for international financial assistance.

The selection of countries was to some extent arbitrary, but the countries included do represent a diversity of situations with respect to geographical region, population size, income level, degree of self-sufficiency, degree of financial constraint, and variation of domestic policy. India was included as an example of a more or less self-sufficient country, but is atypical in that it was previously a large importer and has created a distribution network through which food imports can be channeled if needed. Such networks do not exist in many African countries that are also relatively self-sufficient and need to import only when domestic production fails. See the Appendix for more detail on the methodology and data.

Figure 3 presents the results of simulation experiments for selected countries. It illustrates the relative importance of policies to stabilize prices and to allocate foreign exchange (FE) to food imports. "Restricted FE" and "unrestricted FE" refer to the propensity of the country to restrict the use of foreign exchange for food imports; "market price" means that the domestic price

Figure 3. *Probability of Consumption Falling below 95 Percent of Trend without Any Financial Facility*

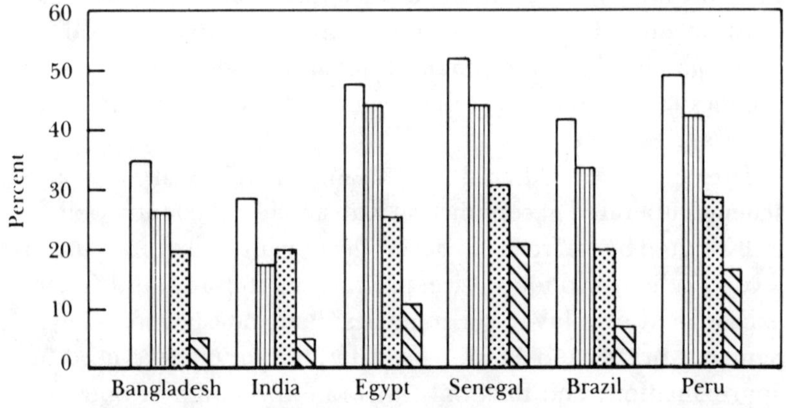

Note: ☐ restricted FE, market price; ▥ restricted FE, stabilized price; ▩ unrestricted FE, market price; ▧ unrestricted FE, stabilized price. "Restricted FE" and "unrestricted FE" refer to the propensity of the country to restrict the use of foreign exchange for food imports. "Market price" means that the domestic price of food fluctuates with the world market price, while "stabilized price" refers to a policy whereby the domestic price of food is insulated from the international price.

of food fluctuates with the world market price, while "stabilized price" refers to a policy whereby the domestic price of food is insulated from the international price. If unstable import prices are transmitted to the domestic market, food insecurity remains high despite the priority given to food imports in allocating foreign exchange. If the propensity to restrict foreign exchange allocations for food imports (*m*) is high, consumption cannot be stabilized during a shortfall in production because the country will not allocate the additional foreign exchange required to import any food needed to cover the shortfall. A high level of food security is possible only through a combination of policies to stabilize domestic prices and a low propensity to restrict foreign exchange allocations for food imports.

Alternative International Financing Facilities

The effect of an international financial arrangement to reduce or eliminate the foreign exchange constraint depends on the degree of instability in the domestic food supply, import prices, and the availability of foreign exchange; the rules governing drawings from the facility; the country's price stabilization policy; and its food import priorities when foreign exchange is scarce. Depending on the combination of circumstances, the effect on food security of a financial facility can range from almost nil to quite large.

Scarcity of foreign exchange may be caused by a rise in the world price of food imports or a decline in domestic food production, so that the desired import bill exceeds the trend level of foreign exchange available for food imports without reducing nonfood imports. Or scarcity may be caused by a shortfall in export earnings or diversion of export earnings to nonfood imports, so that the actual amount of foreign exchange available for food imports is less than the trend amount. Three types of facilities are considered for dealing with food insecurity. The first would allow drawings based solely on shortfalls in foreign exchange availability, the second would cover overruns in the food import bill, and the third would cover both.

*A Facility to Stabilize Available Foreign Exchange (*SAFE)

The SAFE facility would correspond closely to the CFF operated by the IMF before the 1981 decision to broaden coverage to include food imports. It would contribute to food security by raising the availability of foreign exchange when there is a shortfall in export earnings, so that nonfood and food imports could be maintained as long as the value of desired food imports does not exceed the trend value of imports. When the cost of desired imports exceeds the trend value, however, this facility would not assure financing of the full quantity of desired imports.

The IMF facility compensated only for shortfalls in export earnings. Thus, because nonfood imports sometimes varied along with food imports and because drawings were constrained by an upper quota limit, the IMF facility provided less food security than would the simulated SAFE facility.

*A Facility to Stabilize the Food Import Bill (*SFIB)

The SFIB facility would permit countries to draw credits to cover the difference between the actual food import bill and the average food import bill when the former exceeds the latter. This corresponds closely with the proposal for a separate IMF facility to compensate countries for cost overruns in their cereal import bills. In the model the actual food import bill is estimated for given levels of desired food import bills and foreign exchange availability, including potential drawings from the facility. Countries would in general draw credits when the desired food import bill exceeds the average food import bill, except when a reduced amount of available foreign exchange and a high propensity to restrict food imports leads them to reduce food imports below the desired level in spite of the opportunity to draw credits from the facility.

An Integrated Stabilization Facility (INTEG)

The INTEG facility would eliminate all foreign exchange constraints on food imports, whether they are caused by a higher than normal food import bill or by a shortfall in available foreign exchange. Drawings would equal the excess of the desired food import bill over the available foreign exchange for food imports. Thus, this facility would cover both the difference between the desired import bill and the available foreign exchange for food imports and the difference between mean and actual foreign exchange available for food imports. Like the new IMF facility that would integrate compensation for shortfalls in export earnings and for overruns in cereal import costs, INTEG would allow a surplus in export earnings to reduce the coverage for cereal import overruns, and a reduction in cereal import costs to reduce the coverage for shortfalls in export earnings. Thus, this facility would permit countries to fully cover desired food imports and desired consumption, provided that the bill for desired nonfood imports is constant or, if not, that the propensity to restrict foreign exchange expenditure for food imports is high. Unlike the new IMF facility, this scheme is not constrained by quota limits.

Comparison of the Alternative Facilities

Figures 4 and 5 illustate the effect on food security and the expected drawings from the three foreign exchange assistance schemes given two sets of country policies. Country policy A is characterized by low concern with food security: there is no insulation from world market or domestic production fluctuations, prices and consumption levels are unstable irrespective of

Figure 4. *Probability of Consumption Falling below 95 Percent of Trend with Financial Facilities, for Country Policy A*

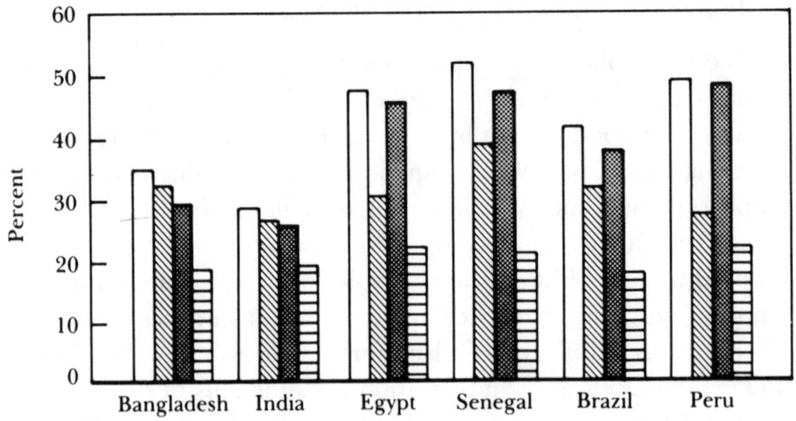

Note: ☐ none; ▧ SAFE; ▩ SFIB; ☰ INTEG. Country policy A is defined in Figure 6.

foreign exchange constraints, and the propensity to restrict foreign exchange allocations for food is high when the value of desired imports is greater than the amount of available foreign exchange. Under country policy B there is relatively high concern about food security: prices to consumers are stabilized, and about half of the shortfall is made up by reducing other imports or by drawing down foreign exchange reserves when the value of desired imports is greater than the amount of foreign exchange available for imports.

The integrated scheme (INTEG), which by definition eliminates any shortfall of foreign exchange, has an impressive effect on food security in both cases. However, food insecurity remains high when the country does not also stabilize internal prices. There are, of course, many reasons why a government may not wish to stabilize aggregate consumption by stabilizing prices, or may find it difficult to do so. One reason may be that the government would be unable to stand by this policy when foreign exchange constraints make it impossible to secure the needed volume of imports. In such cases a government may consider it politically unwise to build up expectations it might not be able to fulfill. Thus a reliable arrangement for international foreign exchange assistance might encourage the adoption of a policy to stabilize prices. For instance, under an INTEG scheme, a country like Peru might be encouraged to reduce the probability of consumption falling below 95 percent of normal from 50 to 3 percent.

Figures 4 and 5 also indicate that the SAFE scheme would have a large effect on food security for countries in which the foreign exchange available for food imports varies more than does the bill for desired food imports. In some cases the SAFE scheme would have a greater effect on security than the SFIB facility.

Food security resulting from an international facility would be much higher if countries would also try to stabilize internal

Figure 5. *Probability of Consumption Falling below 95 Percent of Trend with Financial Facilities, for Country Policy B*

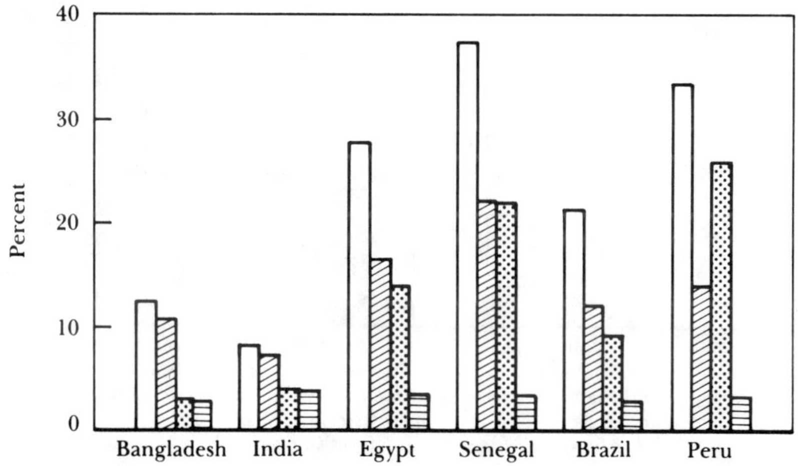

Note: ☐ none; ▨ SAFE; ⚃ SFIB; ☰ INTEG. Country policy B is defined in Figure 6.

prices. This is illustrated in Figure 6, which is based on the average food insecurity calculated for the six countries combined. The graph shows that food security improves dramatically if countries receiving foreign exchange assistance also adopt policies to promote food security.

Figure 6 also illustrates the impressive effectiveness of an export earnings facility such as SAFE. In fact, under an unstable price policy, the effect is larger than that of a separate food import bill facility such as SFIB. But, as might be expected, an integrated approach is the most effective way to reduce unstable food consumption. A change in domestic policy increases stability most dramatically when combined with any of the three facilities, as shown by the last set of bars in the graph.

The expected annual drawings by country from the alternative international schemes are shown in Figure 7, while total expected

Figure 6. *Stabilizing Effect of Financial Facilities on Average Food Consumption*

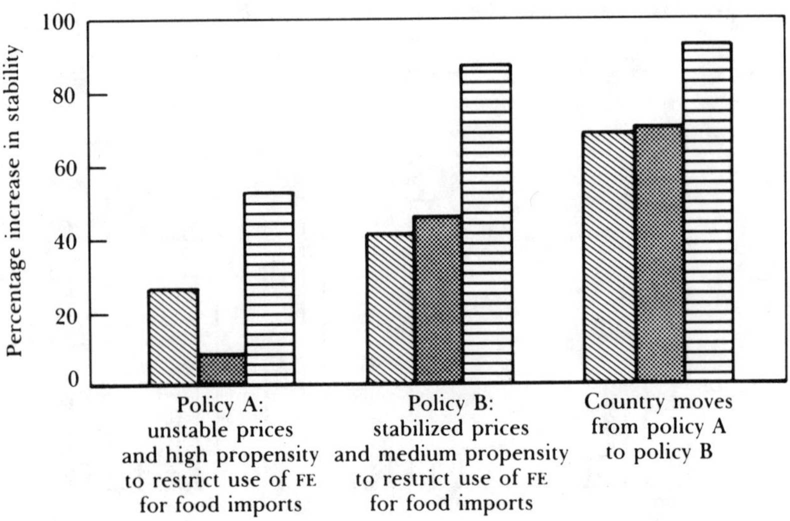

Note: SAFE; SFIB; INTEG. Averages are calculated for six countries: Bangladesh, India, Egypt, Senegal, Brazil, and Peru.

Figure 7. *Expected Annual Drawings of Six Countries from International Financial Facilities*

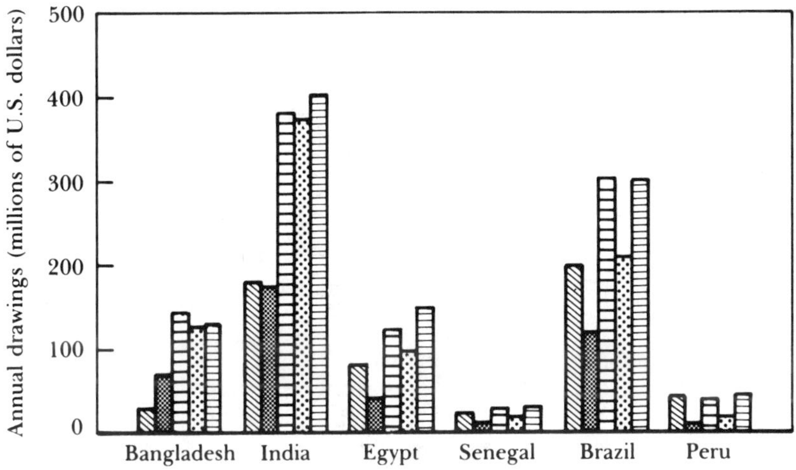

Note: SAFE; policy A, SFIB; policy A, INTEG; policy B, SFIB; policy B, INTEG. Policies A and B are defined in Figure 6.

annual drawings are shown in Figure 8. Drawings from SAFE are unrelated to the country's import policies to promote food security, but expected drawings from INTEG also are not very sensitive to the country's policy. This is in contrast to the large differences in the relative reduction in food insecurity provided by SFIB under different country policies.

The sum of the estimated drawings from the SAFE and SFIB schemes would underestimate the expected total drawings if the two schemes were operated separately. The reason for this is that expected drawings from the SFIB scheme were calculated on the assumption that there was no SAFE facility. If both schemes were in effect, however, the combined expected drawings needed to achieve a given level of food security would be much higher than those for an integrated scheme. For instance, assuming that the countries are pursuing policies to increase food security, the expected drawings from the two separate schemes for India and

Figure 8. *Total Expected Annual Drawings from International Financial Facilities*

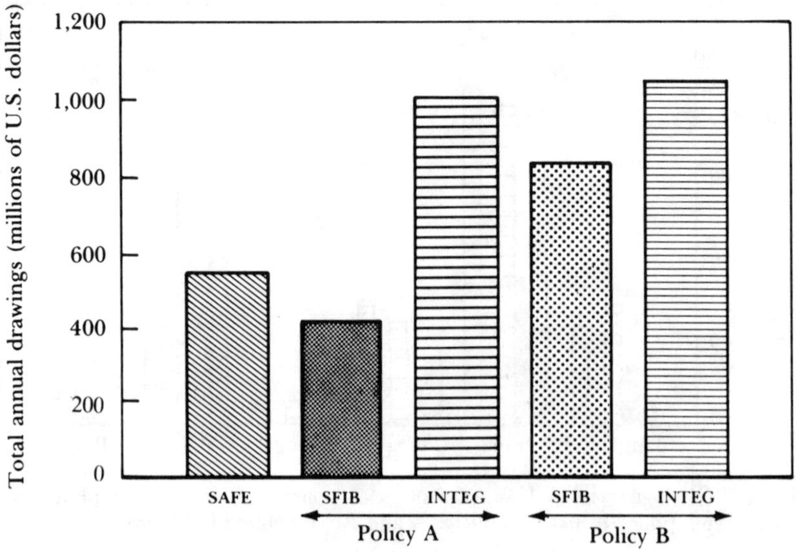

Brazil would exceed US$551 million and US$405 million, respectively, as compared with US$402 million and US$300 million, respectively, from the integrated scheme.

Figures 9, 10, and 11 illustrate why new or expanded foreign exchange assistance schemes might interest major food exporting countries. Under an INTEG scheme, average annual imports by the six countries would increase by from 2.4 million to 5.1 million tons above expected levels without a facility, depending on the domestic price policies. Although these additional imports would not be large in relation to total world supplies or even to total exports, they would represent substantial increases over expected import demand without a facility.

Barring a foreign exchange constraint, policy B implies more imports than policy A when the world price is high, and less

Figure 9. *Expected Imports under Various International Financial Facilities, for Country Policy A*

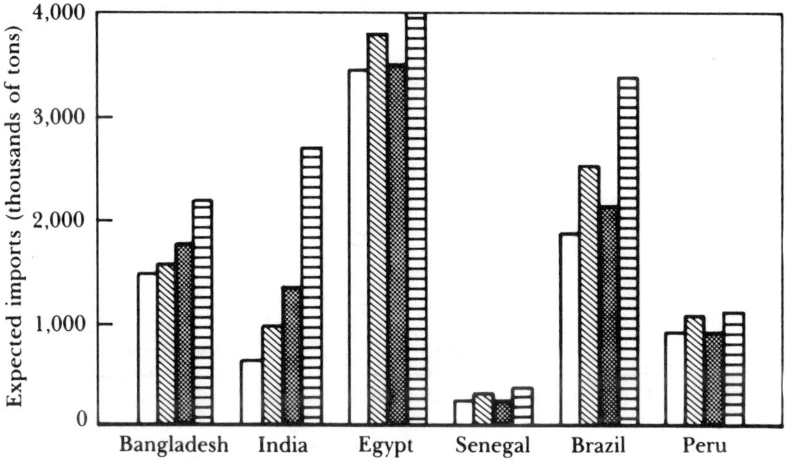

Note: ☐ none; ▨ SAFE; ▩ SFIB; ▤ INTEG. Policy A is defined in Figure 6.

Figure 10. *Expected Imports under Various International Financial Facilities, for Country Policy B*

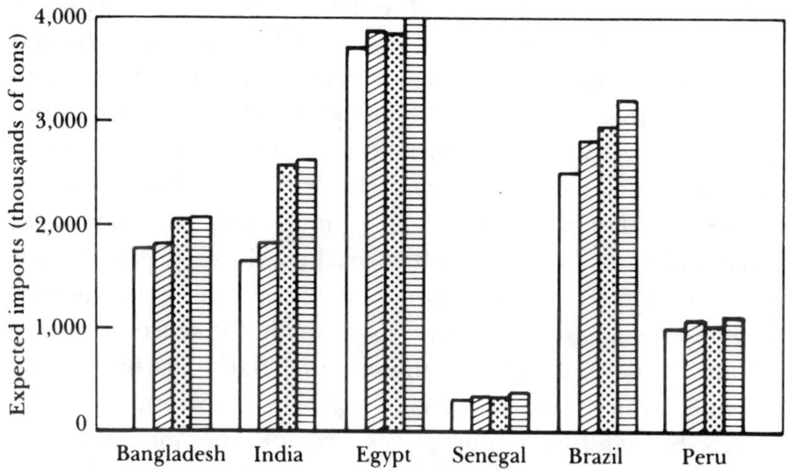

Note: ☐ none; ▨ SAFE; ▩ SFIB; ▤ INTEG. Policy B is defined in Figure 6.

Figure 11. *Total Expected Imports and Additional Imports under Various International Financial Facilities, for Country Policies A and B*

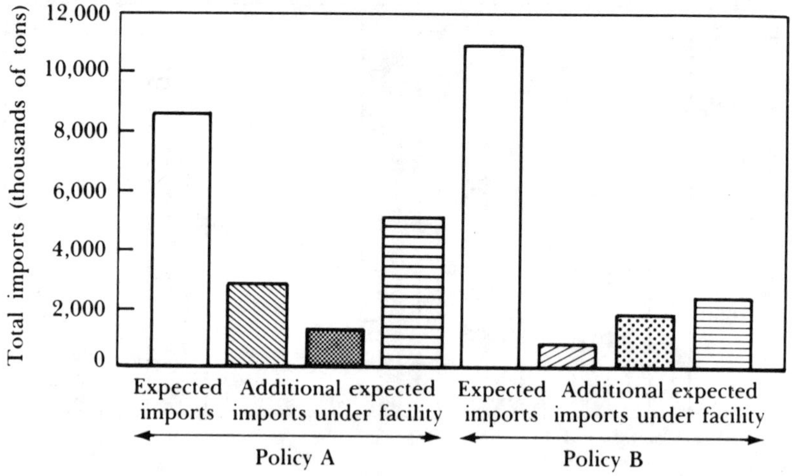

Note: ▧ policy A, SAFE; ▩ policy A, SFIB; ▤ policy A, INTEG; ▨ policy B, SAFE; ▦ policy B, SFIB; ▤ policy B, INTEG. Policies A and B are defined in Figure 6.

imports when the world price is low. In the model, expected overall imports are higher under policy B because the probability of above average prices is higher than the probability of below average prices. In the model that specifies linear demand functions, foreign exchange constraints arising from low export earnings or poor harvests are more likely to keep imports below desired levels under policy A than under policy B. Hence, the SAFE and INTEG schemes, which exclusively or predominantly relax foreign exchange constraints arising from below normal export earnings or poor harvests, provide for more additional imports under policy A than under policy B. Contrarily, the SFIB scheme, which relaxes foreign exchange constraints partly caused by high food import prices, provides for more additional imports under policy B than under policy A.

Clearly, the value of additional imports resulting from a financial facility would be less than the drawings from the financial facility, as countries would have imported part of the deficit anyway. This would be particularly true for countries with a low propensity to restrict the use of foreign exchange for food imports. For such countries, the facility could nevertheless provide important balance of payments relief and prevent economically harmful reductions in nonfood imports occasioned by increases in the food import bill.

For a particular country, the model can predict the likelihood of various intensities of drawings from a financial facility and the resulting increases in cereal imports. Generally, there is a 50 percent or higher chance that the country will not use the facility at all. Figures 12 and 13 show the 10 and 5 percent probabilities, respectively, that drawings will exceed stated

Figure 12. *Drawings from International Financial Facilities in Excess of Stated Amounts at the 10 Percent Level of Probability*

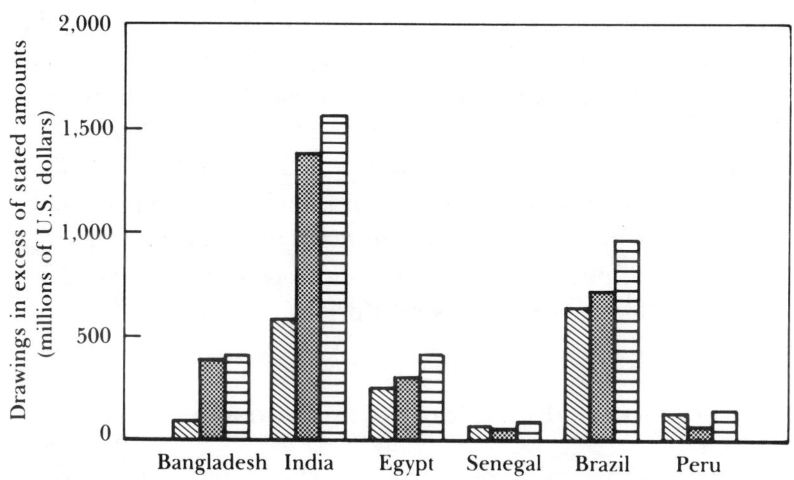

Note: SAFE; SFIB; INTEG.

Figure 13. *Drawings from International Financial Facilities in Excess of Stated Amounts at the 5 Percent Level of Probability*

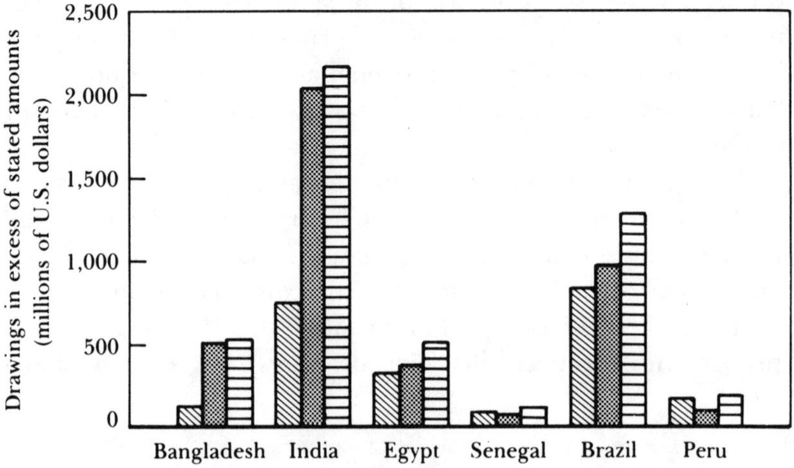

Note: SAFE; SFIB; INTEG.

amounts. These probabilities are based on the assumption that countries pursue a price stabilization policy and give medium priority to allocating scarce foreign exchange for food imports. The probability that the combined drawings of the six countries will exceed the sum of the drawings at the stated levels will be much lower. How much lower depends on how much production shortfalls in the participating countries are correlated and on whether drawings are the consequence of production shortfalls or of a higher than normal world price.

Interaction of Buffer Stocks and Finance

Two other measures frequently discussed in connection with food security are stabilization of domestic and global food supplies. For this discussion, a 50 percent reduction of the standard deviations of domestic and global cereal supplies is postulated. The particular buffer stock arrangements and the size of the stocks required to achieve these levels of stabilization were not considered. Reduction in domestic instability could be achieved through domestically held buffer stocks, while higher global stability could be obtained through some combination of stocks and trade liberalization policies in the major exporting and importing countries. A reduction in the variability of global supplies of such size would imply a reduction in the mean import price

Figure 14. *Indian Food Consumption under Alternate International Financial Facilities*

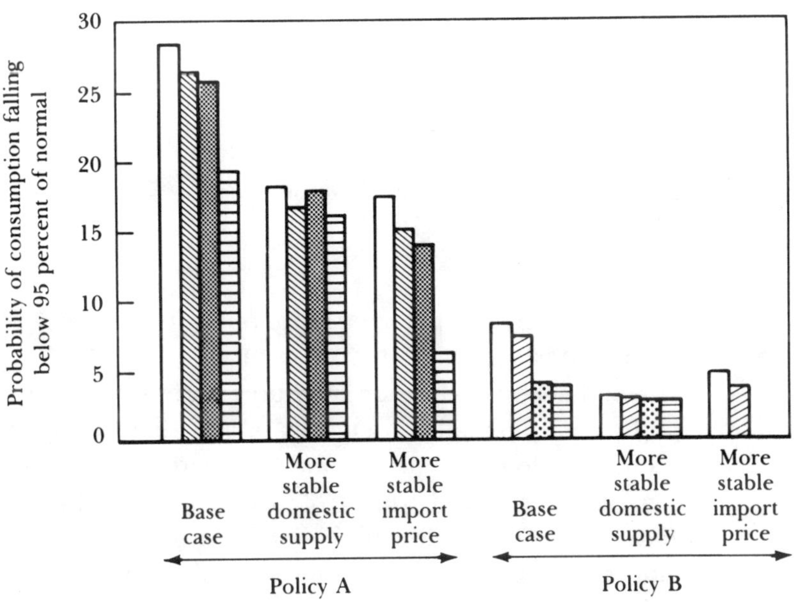

Note: ☐ none; ▧ policy A, SAFE; ▩ policy A, SFIB; ▤ policy A, INTEG; ▨ policy B, SAFE; ⚄ policy B, SFIB; ⊟ policy B, INTEG.

Figure 15. *Brazilian Food Consumption under Alternate International Financial Facilities*

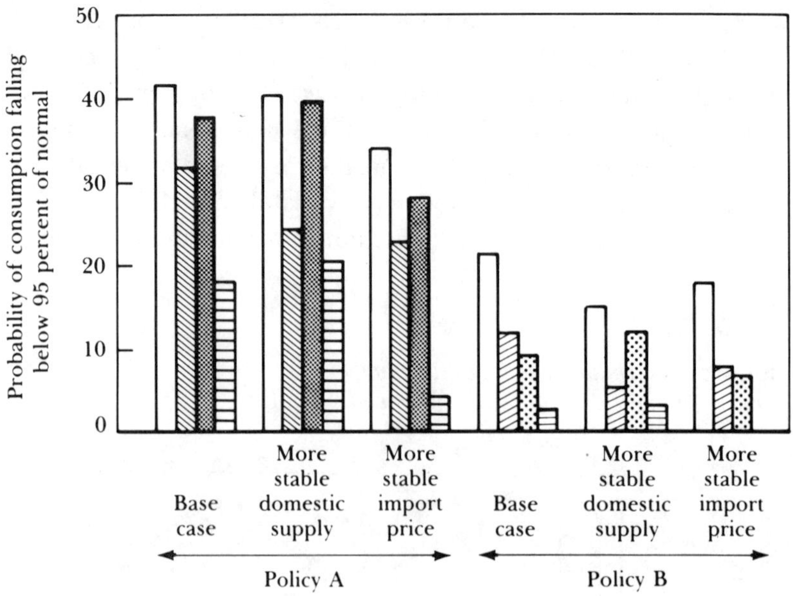

Note: none; policy A, SAFE; policy A, SFIB; policy A, INTEG; policy B, SAFE; policy B, SFIB; policy B, INTEG.

from US$225 to US$215 per metric ton, and its standard deviation from US$50 to US$25 per metric ton.

The effect of such stabilization measures on food security in India and Brazil is illustrated in Figures 14 and 15, respectively. The more stable domestic supply and the more stable import price scenarios correspond with a reduction in the respective standard deviations of 50 percent. As noted earlier, under policy A instability in world prices is transmitted to the domestic market, and there is a high propensity to restrict foreign exchange for food imports. Under country policy B prices are stabilized, and there is a medium propensity to restrict foreign exchange.

In general, even a much more stable domestic food supply or import price would far from eliminate food insecurity if foreign exchange is constraining food imports. But financial schemes to relieve foreign exchange problems would greatly improve food security.

More important, Figures 14 and 15 indicate that financial arrangements to reduce foreign exchange constraints are an effective substitute for the much more costly buffer stock arrangements. For example, for India under country policy A, the base level of consumption instability is reduced from 28 to 19 percent under an INTEG. Without a facility, it would take a large amount of buffer stocks to obtain the same improvement in food security. For Brazil, the base level of consumption instability is reduced from 41 to 18 percent under an INTEG. Without a facility such an improvement is not achievable with even a 50 percent reduction in the instability of supply. The same pattern appears under country policy B, although the stabilized price policy and lower propensity to restrict food imports generally result in less consumption instability. The differences between the two countries may arise in part because foreign exchange earnings comprise a much larger share of total GNP for Brazil, while India is more nearly self-sufficient in food production.

4
An IMF Facility to Finance Excess Food Import Bills

IN RESPONSE TO A JOINT PROPOSAL of the World Food Council and the Food and Agriculture Organization of the United Nations, the IMF began to consider proposals for an international food financing facility in early 1980. After considerable discussion, and with the support of several national and international bodies, the Board of Directors decided in May 1981 to provide such assistance by broadening the terms of reference of the existing CFF for export earnings. In reaching its decision, the IMF board considered two alternatives: one that would fully integrate the food financing facility into the existing CFF and another that would create a separate food financing facility and link it to the existing facility by a joint quota limit.

The Alternative Proposals

Under the first alternative, cereal imports would be treated as negative exports, and countries would be compensated only when there was a net export shortfall. The procedure would resemble the one already used to compensate shortfalls in export earnings, except that excess cereal imports would be added to shortfalls in export earnings to obtain the net amount of the compensable shortfall. Thus if cereal imports were excessively

large and merchandise exports fell below normal, the requirement for extra cereal imports would be treated as a shortfall in net export earnings, and the country would qualify for additional compensation from the CFF. If, however, merchandise exports fell below normal but cereal import requirements were also small, net export earnings might not be short, and the country would not qualify for compensation. This alternative would provide additional balance of payments support linked specifically to cereal import costs, but only at the expense of some support now provided to offset shortfalls in export earnings.

At present, an allotment of special drawing rights (SDRs) is allocated to each member country unconditionally and is used to purchase other members' currencies and in certain transactions with the IMF itself. In addition each country is assigned an SDR quota, which it purchases with its own currency and against which it can borrow according to the rules and regulations of each of the IMF's different accounts and facilities. Normally, borrowings against quota must be repaid within three to five years at moderate interest rates, although some funds offer easier terms to low-income countries with serious payment imbalances. Each fund or facility within the IMF places an upper limit on the amount that can be borrowed. This limit is expressed as a percentage of the country's quota. For the export earnings facility the limit has been 100 percent of quota.

According to the proposal to integrate a cereal component into the existing CFF, the export earnings component and the cereal component would each be subject to a separate quota limit, and the net amount would be subject to a limit lower than the sum of the two. Both the quota limits and the "netting out" procedure that determines the compensable amount would restrict how much countries could draw.

The second alternative would retain the CFF unchanged and would create a separate food financing facility, which would operate under a joint quota limit applicable to combined drawings from both. Countries could draw from the CFF as they do

now, subject to the existing quota limit of 100 percent. They could also draw from the new food financing facility, which would compensate them for the amount that actual cereal import costs exceed the trend for the year of the drawing. These drawings would also be subject to a limit of from 50 to 100 percent of quota. If countries were eligible for drawings from both facilities in the same year, the combined total of these drawings would be limited to from 125 to 150 percent of quota. This alternative would allow countries to treat separately their requirements for compensation arising from export earnings shortfalls and those

Table 8. *Hypothetical Withdrawals from the Food Financing Facility under the Two Alternative Proposals*
(millions of SDRs)

Item			*Basic data*			
Export shortfall	29	29	29	0	−11	−11
Cereal import excess	14	−16	0	14	14	−16
Calculation of export component: lesser of export shortfall or 100 percent of quota[a]	20	20	20	0	0	0
Calculation of cereal component: lesser of cereal import excess or 100 percent of quota[a]	14	0	0	14	14	0
			Integrated approach			
Sum of export and cereal components (A)	34	20	20	14	14	0
or						
Net export shortfall (B)	43	13	29	14	3	0
Drawing equals the lesser of (A) or (B) with a quota limit of 125 percent[a]	25	13	20	14	3	0
			Separate approach			
Sum of export and cereal component (A) with a quota limit of 125 percent[a]	25	20	20	14	14	0

a. Where 100 percent of quota equals 20 million SDRs.
Source: Constructed by authors from hypothetical data.

from excess cereal import costs. The joint quota limit would prevent a country from making extremely high withdrawals from both facilities in the same year. The difference between the two approaches is shown in the hypothetical example in Table 8.

Estimated Aggregate Drawings

If there were no quota limits, aggregate drawings would differ considerably under the two alternatives considered by the IMF. Without constraints, the second alternative, which allows for full compensation for both export shortfalls and cereal import excesses, results in a significantly higher aggregate level of drawings because the drawings from the food facility are in addition to drawings from the CFF. Under the first alternative, countries that have a high correlation between the value of merchandise exports and the cereal import bill would not receive the full additional benefit of the new facility because their cereal drawings would be constrained by their export excesses, and their export earnings drawings would be constrained by low cereal import bills. A separate food facility would allow these countries to receive the full amount for which they are eligible from both facilities.

When quota limits are introduced, aggregate drawings under both alternatives are sharply reduced, but the second still results in a somewhat higher total than the first. The quota limit strongly inhibits drawings from the existing CFF for export earnings but does not have much effect on drawings to fully compensate countries for excess cereal import costs. Thus, with quota limits, the main difference between the two alternatives is that there is less than full compensation for cereal import excesses because of the offsetting effect of export surpluses under the first alternative, as opposed to full compensation under the second one. As a rough approximation, additional annual average drawings for cereal imports in a noncrisis year might amount to 100 million

SDRs under a fully integrated scheme and 390 million under a separate scheme with joint quota limits. In a crisis year these amounts could rise to 590 million and 730 million, respectively, for the two alternatives.

Limitations and Benefits of a Food Financing Facility

Under either approach an IMF food financing facility would provide balance of payments support only when the costs of cereal imports rise sharply. Concern for the consumption shortfalls of developing countries in periods when domestic production was short and world prices were high led to interest in creating such a facility. But maintaining minimum levels of per capita consumption for all segments of a country's population is beyond the purview of an international financial institution. Many countries cannot fully implement domestic policies to maintain minimum consumption for everyone until they achieve full employment and minimum income standards for all wage earners. These countries will require consumption subsidies or targeted food distribution programs to counter chronic malnutrition for vulnerable groups for the foreseeable future. Such food subsidy programs are better supported by grants of food aid and other highly concessional resource transfers than by a balance of payment facility. These transfers enable countries to finance immediate consumption needs of low-income groups without diverting resources from productive investment.

Despite these limitations, balance of payments support for excess cereal import costs can serve a number of useful purposes. A financial facility can relieve many developing countries of foreign exchange constraints, such as those that occurred in the mid-1970s when price instability increased. The facility could enable them to bid competitively for the food imports needed to meet effective demand in years of scarcity.

For countries that do not now attempt to stabilize domestic cereal prices, a food financing facility could provide a cushion that would enable them to introduce such policies. For countries that currently try to stabilize prices for urban consumers but allow prices to fluctuate sharply in rural areas, financial support for extra imports in years of domestic production shortfall could provide an incentive to develop rural procurement and marketing programs that would channel additional imports to rural consumers.

Finally, for countries that try to stabilize prices and consumption by allowing nonfood imports to drop when cereal import costs increase, a food financing facility could help maintain a smooth flow of investment into infrastructure development and productive enterprise. Although the effect of the facility on levels of cereal imports may not be very great in such cases, the overall economic benefit may be considerable. It would allow the country to achieve the longer run economic goals that make adequate consumption levels possible.

It seems likely that low-income countries generally will gain relatively more from a food financing facility because fluctuations in the costs of cereal imports are a more important balance of payments problem for them than for middle-income countries. In addition, low-income countries cannot readily borrow on short notice in international capital markets at average lending rates, whereas most middle-income countries can and do borrow extensively in the private capital market. The benefits would be greater for low-income countries that have a policy to stabilize food consumption and a low marginal propensity to restrict foreign exchange expenditures for food imports. Even though some low-income countries could not make full use of the proposed facility in the immediate future, it would establish a cushion against future needs.

One consideration that could be increasingly important during the next decade is the role of noncereal items in the total food

Table 9. *Composition of the Gross Food Import Bill for Selected Countries, 1961–65, 1968–72, and 1976–78*
(percent)

Region and country	*Period*	*Wheat*	*Rice*	*Other cereals*	*Non-cereals*
Asia					
Bangladesh	1961–65	33	30	0	37
	1968–72	42	28	0	30
	1976–78	41	22	0	36
India	1961–65	68	22	2	9
	1968–72	53	24	3	19
	1976–78	39	5	2	54
Indonesia	1961–65	7	88	1	5
	1968–72	19	67	3	11
	1976–78	8	66	1	25
Philippines	1961–65	28	32	0	40
	1968–72	34	11	2	52
	1976–78	47	2	8	43
Sri Lanka	1961–65	13	38	0	48
	1968–72	29	29	0	42
	1976–78	51	32	0	17
North Africa/Middle East					
Egypt	1961–65	64	0	8	28
	1968–72	59	0	2	39
	1976–78	50	0	7	43
Jordan	1961–65	29	11	2	57
	1968–72	21	6	3	70
	1976–78	20	5	6	69
Somalia	1961–65	11	37	6	46
	1968–72	20	35	8	36
	1976–78	13	21	14	53
Syria	1961–65	18	11	1	70
	1968–72	37	8	0	55
	1976–78	25	9	2	64

Region and country	*Period*	*Wheat*	*Rice*	*Other cereals*	*Non-cereals*
Sub-Saharan Africa					
Mali	1961–65	10	0	2	87
	1968–72	11	21	10	58
	1976–78	16	14	9	60
Senegal	1961–65	12	33	5	50
	1968–72	15	34	6	45
	1976–78	17	38	8	37
Tanzania	1961–65	19	11	13	56
	1968–72	11	7	14	68
	1976–78	15	21	14	50
Upper Volta	1961–65	19	13	1	67
	1968–72	36	3	0	61
	1976–78	26	17	10	47
Latin America					
Bolivia	1961–65	57	2	0	41
	1968–72	56	0	0	44
	1976–78	63	0	0	37
Brazil	1961–65	83	0	1	16
	1968–72	64	0	2	34
	1976–78	56	2	10	33
Chile	1961–65	29	3	1	67
	1968–72	21	4	8	66
	1976–78	60	2	5	33
Haiti	1961–65	43	0	0	57
	1968–72	31	0	0	68
	1976–78	32	13	2	53
Peru	1961–65	49	7	1	43
	1968–72	47	3	1	48
	1976–78	47	5	13	35

Note: Food is broadly defined to include meats, dairy products, cereals, fruits and vegetables, sugar, pulses, root crops, oil seeds and vegetable oil, cocoa beans, and derivatives.

Source: Data compiled by Grant Scobie and Alberto Valdés, IFPRI.

import bill. For many countries noncereal foods, particularly vegetable oils and sugar, comprise a significant proportion of the diet of poor people and of the total food import bill. When minimum requirements for cereal protein have been satisfied, these two items are among the first to be added to a diet to provide extra calories and nutritional balance. For many low-income countries, these items are important dietary necessities for the poor, not just luxury goods for the middle classes.

On average, noncereal items accounted for more than 40 percent of total food imports for ten of eighteen developing countries between 1976 and 1978 (Table 9). Therefore, it seems worthwhile for the IMF to consider a broader definition of food. One possible approach would be to define the basic food basket of the poor in each country and to determine the food import bill in relation to the items required to meet that minimum demand. Such a basket would differ from country to country.

Justification for the Alternative Selected

In examining the two alternatives considered by the IMF, a good argument can be made in favor of the first, in which excess cereal imports are treated as negative exports. Although the second provides a larger absolute level of benefits with the same quota limits, it is not clear that countries really need help with their balance of payments when the excess cost of cereal imports is offset by an increase in the value of merchandise exports. From the standpoint of food security, the food financing facility can make its most important contribution in years of extreme hardship when cereal prices are high, export revenues are low, and import requirements are above normal.

In normal years the first approach gives considerably less compensation than the second, but in crisis years, such as 1974 and 1975, both provide comparable levels of assistance. Thus, the integrated facility would seem to be a better use of IMF resources and would provide good coverage with relatively liberal quota limits. With quota limits of 100 percent for both the export and the cereal components of an integrated scheme and a combined limit of 125 percent, credit availability to low-income countries could increase by up to 15 percent above outstanding IMF drawings for this group in mid-1979. This takes into account the repayment provisions that would call for repurchase of drawing rights in equal installments in the fourth and fifth years following the drawing.

This alternative was adopted by the IMF Board of Directors in May 1981. IMF members can choose whether to participate in the new food financing facility. If a country believes it will benefit more from continuing to participate in the CFF under the old rules, it may choose to do so. Once an option has been selected, however, it may not be changed for three years. Payments for a member's excess cereal imports are to be based on data for the latest twelve-month period, but if timely data cannot be obtained during a food crisis, cereal imports may be estimated for up to twelve months ahead and provision made for rapid repayment of excess drawings, if any. As with the export earnings facility, a member must demonstrate that it has a balance of payments need, that the excess in cereal imports results from circumstances largely beyond its control, and that it will cooperate with the IMF to seek appropriate solutions for its balance of payments difficulties. The facility will operate for an initial period of four years with an evaluation after two years.

The facility adopted is compatible with other forms of food security assistance, particularly food aid. Because food aid is relatively more available in normal years and is considerably more concessional than the food financing facility, it would presumably be the preferred form of assistance. In a crisis situation, however, food aid supplies are likely to decrease as prices climb, and countries' needs for alternative balance of payments support would increase proportionately.

The question of accounting for food aid flows in establishing the amount to be compensated by the food financing facility will be a potentially troublesome issue. It need not be difficult, however, if the cost of food aid is counted as zero in the year of the drawing, in the same way that the cost of the IMF drawing itself entails no foreign exchange expenditure in the year it is obtained. Thus, excess cereal import costs would be calculated against the actual foreign-exchange expenditure for commercial cereal imports plus the transport costs for food aid. On the one hand, if food aid in that year dropped sharply and the cost of commercial cereal imports rose steeply as a consequence, that increase could be fully compensated by the food financing facility. On the other hand, if food aid rose significantly in response to an unusual need, the country could not receive help from this plan for the amount covered by food aid. In the longer term, adjustments to variations in food aid flows and food import requirements would have to be worked out through normal adjustments in the country's balance of payments.

Determination of Need

The overall objectives of the facility are very clear. It will provide assistance only when import bills are above normal and are not offset by favorable export earnings; they must be temporary and largely attributable to circumstances beyond the control of the government requesting assistance. However, distinguishing what is a situation attributable to circumstances beyond government control from one that is the result of domestic policies is sometimes a complex task.

The method for calculating drawings—based on deviations from a five-year moving average—implies a built-in adjustment mechanism to reflect changes in the trend level of imports. If the excess food import bill lasts for a single year, aside from quota limits on drawings, the effect of the excess cereal import bill on the net import capacity (net of export earnings) can be largely offset by the drawings from the facility. If the increase in the food import bill were to last for several years, the "excess" as defined to measure import requirements would progressively disappear. Under such circumstances, the country might apply for financial assistance from the IMF for balance of payments difficulties, usually under requirements of cooperation with the IMF in implementing policy adjustments.[1] Thus, over the years, governments requesting financial assistance from the facility to cover additional imports to offset production shortfalls resulting from inappropriate domestic policies would not benefit relatively more than others. During the first and perhaps the second year of a production shortfall, however, to the extent that it is difficult for the IMF to determine in practice whether the shortfall is attributable to circumstances beyond the government's control, there is a possibility of some abuse of the scheme, but it would be short-lived.

A different case arises when additional imports are the result of increases in the levels of domestic stocks rather than a production shortfall. Holding stocks is in itself an expensive operation, and it is hard to find cases of "overinvestment" in buffer stocks of cereals in developing countries with food shortages. For countries that have a buffer stocks policy, it is a positive feature of the facility that it allows for more flexibility to expand imports in years when import prices are low. But it is not anticipated that the creation of the facility will induce larger levels of stocks in countries with food shortages.[2]

1. A similar situation has been well illustrated for the facility on export revenues in Louis Goreux, *Compensatory Financing Facility,* Pamphlet Series no. 34 (Washington, D.C.: International Monetary Fund, 1980).

2. For an empirical analysis showing the relation between domestically held stocks and financial assistance, see John McIntire, *Food Security in the Sahel: Variable Import Levy, Grain Reserves, and Foreign Exchange Assistance,* Research Report no. 26 (Washington, D.C.: International Food Policy Research Institute, 1981).

A question has arisen as to whether the IMF should apply "conditionality" to the use of the facility: that is, should it impose conditions regarding domestic distribution and consumption stabilization policies which governments must follow. Imposing conditionality in the form of policies to stabilize domestic consumption raises difficult practical and normative issues. Is it practical? How could the IMF expect to know what should and could realistically be done in each case without hiring an army of experts to continually examine each country's program of action? It would be very expensive, the political environment in many developing countries would make it difficult to respond positively to the conditions, and it would have dubious results, even if implemented. The dialogue about correct policies is better carried on in a larger context of relations with the World Bank, the Food and Agriculture Organization, and bilateral aid donors. The facility can, however, help to implement such policies. Years of food shortages are not the appropriate time to delay assistance while domestic policies are investigated. The test of cooperation for borrowing under the facility should not go beyond the determination of need in the sense of an actual or expected increase in the food import bill from causes beyond the government's control.

Effect on the Use of Forward Contracts

There is no explicit restriction in the IMF rules that prevents the use of futures markets. In fact, the facility gives more financial flexibility to take advantage of the cheapest way to buy. There are, however, two considerations, which in some cases could limit the use of futures markets. First, countries expecting to receive food aid—primarily low-income countries—might be reluctant to buy contracts in the futures markets if these operations affect the donor's allocations of food aid to them. But it is the uncertainty about the food aid allocations rather than the rules of the financial facility which may actually prevent buying in futures markets.

Second, to determine the compensation for commercial imports under the facility, the IMF uses customs data and thus would not count imports until the grain actually arrives in the country. The IMF could, however, give a loan to cover the food import deficit up to six months into the future, with the understanding that the account would be settled between the importing country and the IMF when the grain is delivered. Thus, funds from the facility could be used to finance forward contracts. For some countries, forward contracts offer an attractive alternative to acquiring and storing reserve stocks, which access to a facility may make easier to implement. However, the circumstances of other countries may dictate other choices.[3]

3. For elaboration of this point, see Richard Gilmore and Barbara Huddleston, "The Food Security Challenge," *Food Policy*, vol. 8, no. 1 (February 1983), pp. 33–46.

5
Effects of the IMF Facility on International Market Prices

THE DEBATE ON CREATION of the food financing facility raised several questions about its possible effect on world grain prices. Some think that the financial facility could create a significant increase in demand by developing countries for grain in some years and thus could put strong pressure on prices to rise. But if the facility covers only excess foreign exchange costs of cereal imports without affecting domestic consumption, the increase in demand generated by the facility would not be very great.

In its early deliberations, the IMF made it clear that it did not have an institutional mandate to subsidize programs to increase consumption or to improve nutrition in developing countries. All it could appropriately offer would be financing to countries whose foreign exchange positions were strained by the extra pressure of high cereal import bills in certain years when normal consumption could not be maintained without additional cost. Nor do the IMF calculations based on the historical period provide for any increase in demand above the amounts of grain actually imported during the period. Thus in 1966, 1967, and 1968, and again in 1974 and 1975, years in which the real value of cereal imports for developing countries as a whole exceeded the five-year moving average, a food facility would have been liable for that excess value, but would not have created additional demand beyond what was actually satisfied in those years. Using

Table 10. *Actual and Trend Volumes and Values of Cereal Imports in Developing Countries, 1965 to 1976*

	Value (billions of 1977) U.S. dollars)		*Volume (millions of metric tons)*		*Wheat price (in real terms, 1977 U.S. dollars)*
Year	*Trend (deflated)*	*Actual (deflated)*	*Trend*	*Actual*	
1965	3.16	2.98	37.3	36.0	144.5
1966	3.33	3.41	38.8	41.4	153.3
1967	3.31	3.55	38.5	40.3	149.3
1968	3.40	3.57	39.5	40.2	151.3
1969	3.43	3.03	39.6	34.6	144.1
1970	3.44	3.44	40.2	41.0	131.6
1971	4.13	3.54	43.2	42.2	132.4
1972	6.06	3.62	48.3	42.9	133.1
1973	7.80	7.02	52.0	55.1	218.9
1974	9.19	12.69	55.0	60.5	227.6
1975	10.54	12.11	59.0	59.1	153.3
1976	11.73	10.53	62.9	57.2	134.5

Source: FAO trade tapes and IFPRI calculations.

data from the Food and Agriculture Organization on imports for 101 developing countries, the International Food Policy Research Institute has calculated that the sum of the aggregate excess cereal import bill for 1965 to 1976 would be US$5.5 billion in 1977 dollars (see Table 10). The IMF staff arrived at a figure of about 1 billion SDRs for an integrated scheme with quota limits and from 2 to 4 billion SDRs for a separate scheme with quota limits.

Likelihood of Increased Demand

Though empirical results still are preliminary, work done by Philip Abbott and Grant Scobie indicates that in most developing countries demand for cereal imports is quite inelastic with respect to world price.[1] Certainly this seems to be true for countries that primarily import wheat for urban consumption. As pointed out above, relieving the strain of high cereal import costs on their overall balance of payments position is a more likely effect than increasing planned levels of cereal imports.

What cannot be predicted, however, is how much countries will modify domestic consumption policies and import practices, knowing that the IMF facility will provide a safety net against unexpected cost increases. Some countries may decide, for example, that they can afford to institute programs to subsidize consumption for a broader spectrum of low-income groups. With assured financing they can sustain such programs with imports in the event of domestic production shortfalls. Others may decide to take advantage of the facility to increase their cereal imports in years of relatively low prices, using the financial assistance provided by the IMF to create domestic food reserves on which they could draw when world market prices are high. Either of these policies could result in increases in demand for cereal imports by developing countries beyond what could be predicted from past trends.

In the simulation reported in Chapter 3, the six countries in Table 12 (in the Appendix) account for more than 40 percent of the population of all developing market economies. Assuming that these six countries would also account for 40 percent of additional import demand created by the facility and taking the integrated scheme as the one most comparable with the IMF facility actually adopted, expected additional demand for all developing countries in a given year would be from 6 million to 13 million tons. The assumption that demand increases will be highly correlated with population is perhaps too strong, how-

1. Philip C. Abbott, "Modeling International Grain Trade with Government Controlled Markets," *American Journal of Agricultural Economics*, vol. 61 (February 1979), pp. 22–31; Grant M Scobie, *Government Policy and Food Imports: The Case of Wheat in Egypt*, Research Report no. 29 (Washington, D.C.: International Food Policy Research Institute, 1981).

ever, because unmet consumption requirements vary from one country to another.

Another calculation estimates the amount of additional demand that would be created if all developing-country importers used the facility to help pursue policies to stabilize consumption. If countries had imported the additional quantities required to maintain per capita consumption at 1961–65 levels through 1978, the aggregate amount would have ranged from a low of 5 million tons in 1969 to a high of 19.2 million tons in 1973 (see Table 11). As pointed out, quota limits do not place a significant constraint on drawings for cereal imports, although they do affect the export component of an integrated facility. Thus these numbers could represent realistic limits for the additional demand that the facility could generate under both normal and abnormal world market conditions.

A first step in understanding the possible effect of such increases in demand is to compare them with the level of world grain imports without the facility. As Table 11 indicates, additional imports by developing countries would have exceeded 10 percent of total world imports in only four out of eighteen years from 1961 through 1978 had the facility been operating then. Thus, the hypothesis that the facility would have a greater effect on price in some years than in others seems borne out by the variability observed in the hypothetical demand requirements for the recent past.

Imports might not increase in the year when additional import requirements are greatest from the standpoint of stabilizing consumption. Countries with variable import requirements and some domestic storage capacity could take advantage of the facility by importing above-trend amounts in years when prices were low and storing the extra grain for use in years when greater domestic need coincided with higher world prices. Whether using the facility for forward buying is more efficient than waiting until a combination of unmet internal demand and high world prices force reliance on IMF credit depends on whether the ex-

Table 11. *Actual Volumes of World and Developing-Country Cereal Imports and Unmet Developing-Country Requirements, 1961 to 1978*

Year	*World total (million metric tons)*	*Developing country total (million metric tons)*	*Additional imports required to maintain per capita consumption at 1961–65 level in developing countries*[a] *(million metric tons)*	*Ratio of additional import requirement in developing countries to world total (percent)*
1961	72.5	29.0	8.5	12
1962	83.5	30.3	5.3	6
1963	83.2	32.8	5.1	6
1964	97.8	36.1	5.2	5
1965	95.0	36.0	17.3	18
1966	110.7	41.1	17.0	15
1967	103.4	40.3	5.1	5
1968	96.9	40.2	8.1	8
1969	89.1	34.6	5.0	6
1970	96.9	41.0	7.9	8
1971	109.2	42.2	8.7	8
1972	109.7	42.9	9.5	9
1973	134.3	55.1	19.2	14
1974	142.4	60.5	9.2	6
1975	135.8	59.1	8.6	6
1976	152.5	57.2	7.4	5
1977	156.0	63.1	12.3	8
1978	166.5	74.6	7.3	4

a. Importing countries with an additional import requirement greater than one million tons were: 1961 Egypt, Morocco, and Turkey; 1962 Bangladesh; 1963 none; 1964 Brazil; 1965 India and Indonesia; 1966 Bangladesh, Brazil, India, Morocco, and Nigeria; 1967 Indonesia and Nigeria; 1968 Nigeria and Turkey; 1969 Egypt; 1970 Egypt and Nigeria; 1971 Bangladesh and Nigeria; 1972 Bangladesh and Nigeria; 1973 Egypt, Nigeria, and Turkey; 1974 Kampuchea and Nigeria; 1975 Nigeria; 1976 Nigeria; 1977 Bangladesh and Nigeria; and 1978 Ethiopia and Vietnam. China is not included in the calculation of the additional import requirement because of the lack of reliable consumption data. Chinese imports, ranging from four to twelve million metric tons per year, are included in the totals for the world and the developing countries.

Source: FAO trade tapes and IFPRI calculations.

pected storage cost is higher than the expected price increase in a crisis year. Although the facility would allow developing countries to obtain desired imports no matter what the price, higher prices would reduce the balance of payments benefits and raise the cost. If the facility created significant additional demand for grain imports in a year when the world balance of supply and demand was already precarious, and if this demand triggered sharp price increases such as those experienced in 1973 to 1975, much of the intended benefit could be negated.

Determinants of the World Price of Wheat

No model of world wheat trade has been developed that can be effectively used to test the possible effect of the food facility on prices. However, a number of experiments have been made with different specifications of the world wheat economy that enable us to make some remarks about the determinants of world price with a fair degree of confidence. Other authors have shown a nonlinear relation between wheat price, cereal stocks, and demand, in which sufficiently large stocks can absorb the shocks of production shortfalls and insulate prices.

T. N. Barr has developed a model of demand and price determination for the United States for 1960 to 1971.[2] Price is a function of the ratio of normal demand to ending stocks, in which stocks increase in importance as they are drawn down. For the United States, minimum working or pipeline stocks for 1973 were considered to be about 200 million bushels, which amounts to a little less than 40 percent of the domestic demand of 520 million bushels. The estimated effects of exogenous stock changes on prices are small, provided that the stocks amount to more than 400 million to 500 million bushels. Barr's specification

2. T. N. Barr, "Demand and Price Relationships for the U.S. Wheat Economy," *Wheat Situation*, No. WS225 (August 1973).

tracked prices well for 1960–71. For 1972–73 the estimated farm wheat price was US$1.78 per bushel compared with the actual price of US$1.80. Simulations from 1964 forward track well for 1964–72, and alternate assumptions permit high prices for 1973. For 1973–74 the model estimated a price of US$3.90, whereas simulations under alternate assumptions regarding exports yielded prices ranging from US$3.07 to $4.01 per bushel. The model also predicted a price of US$2.10 in 1974–75. Warner points out that Barr failed to consider explicitly the relation of market prices to government loan rates, which might affect the model during other periods.[3]

Appendix 3 to IFPRI Research Report no. 4 relates world wheat prices to world cereal demand for 1960–75.[4] Two approaches are used. In the first, a simple linear equation explains price as a function of the imports of developing countries with food deficits, which is a variable demand element. This estimate yields an R^2 of 0.67. A second approach detrends variations in prices and imports and adds the effects of carry-over stocks as represented by lagged price. This is estimated as a nonlinear relation:

$$P_t/P^* = f\,(M_t/\overline{M}_t),\ \ln\,(P_{t-1}/P^*)$$

where P^* is the average world price before 1972, and $\overline{M}_t$ is trend imports of cereals in the food-deficit developing countries. A random variable is introduced to account for shocks such as sudden changes in Soviet demand. The R^2 is increased to 0.75, and the equation is used to simulate prices based on exogenous demand determinations. For 1980 and thereafter, the equation generates an expected price of $155.80, per metric ton, expressed in 1977 dollars.

3. Dennis Lee Warner, "An Econometric Model of the World Wheat Economy," Ph.D. dissertation, Princeton University, Princeton, N.J., 1979.

4. Panos Konandreas, Barbara Huddleston, and Virabongsa Ramangkura, *Food Security: An Insurance Approach*, Research Report no. 4 (Washington, D.C.: International Food Policy Research Institute, 1978).

Gerard Adams and Jere Behrman developed a general commodity model to determine supply, demand, and prices for the world for 1955–71.[5] Wheat price is a function of the ratio of stocks to demand, time, and the imports of centrally planned economies. This specification provides a high R^2. Simulations on price are fair to good. This model supports the hypothesis that stocks, not price, absorb shocks. Simulations based on 5 percent changes in supply or demand in 1956 show little change in simulated prices after one year, and the immediate effect also is not great. The model does not consider consumer and producer responses to price expectations. Estimated long-run elasticity of price to the ratio of stock to demand is -0.16 with a one-year lag in response to exogenous supply or demand shifts, and an average decline in world prices of 4.0 percent a year.

Warner's model of the world wheat economy provides estimates for 1948–74 and simulations for 1960–73.[6] Regional supply and demand submodels are generated, and closure comes through the simultaneous solution of exports, imports, and world prices; import prices essentially follow regional export prices. The basic simulation misses the 1973 price jump, in part because the model does not adequately explain stocking behavior in North America. Basic price simulations for earlier years are strong, and in alternative simulations prices for 1973 are forced up by modifying the model with exogenous drawdowns of stocks.

Predicted Effect of the Facility

For this study we specified a nonlinear function in which the world export price for wheat is a function of the ratio of world stocks to world demand and a time trend (see the Appendix for

5. Gerard F. Adams and Jere R. Behrman, *Econometric Models of World Agricultural Commodity Markets* (Cambridge, Mass.: Ballinger Publishing Company, 1976).
6. Warner, "An Econometric Model of the World Wheat Economy."

the methodology). The results show both a significant declining trend in real world wheat prices and a significant relation between changes in the ratio of stocks to demand and the export price for wheat, particularly as the ratio dropped below 19 percent (see Figure 16).

The equation estimates only the short-term effect on prices of a change in the relation between supply and demand in a given year. With production fixed in the short term, elasticity of supply will depend on stocks. The specification is ex post and uses ending stocks and demand for a specific year to determine the price for that year. However, ending stocks serve here as a proxy for supply; that is, beginning stocks plus production. By using known data for beginning stocks and estimated data for

Figure 16. *Relation of Ratio of Stocks to Demand and World Price of Wheat, Net of Time Trend*

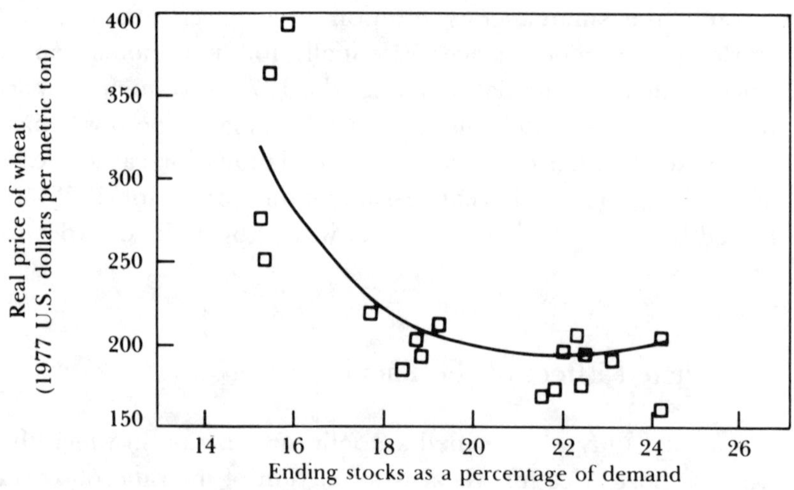

Note: □ actual values, net of estimated time trend; —— estimated values, net of time trend.

Sources: Real prices, World Bank, *Commodity Trade and Price Trends* (Washington, D.C., 1979); stocks and demand, U.S. Department of Agriculture, Foreign Agricultural Service, *Foreign Agricultural Circular—Grains*, FG-28-81 (July 1981); stock data are adjusted using IFPRI data for ending stocks of China.

production and subtracting estimated demand from their sum, an estimated ratio of ending stocks to demand can be obtained for each following year, and with it an indication of price behavior, assuming demand behaves normally.

The equation tells us that an increase in world demand for imports triggered by shortfalls in domestic production will not have much effect on price if beginning stocks are high and can be drawn down without causing the ratio of ending stocks to demand to fall below 17 to 20 percent. This was so throughout the 1960s, when the ratio always exceeded 20 percent, and real price was remarkably stable. The ratio of stocks to demand was less than 19 percent throughout the 1970s, however, and fell below 16 percent in 1973–76 with concomitant variability in world price. Except when the ratio exceeds 19 to 20 percent, the financial facility will be operating in a time of potentially unstable prices, and the effect of additional demand on prices will depend importantly on the size of stocks when the demand increase occurs. As long as world grain reserves are adequate, any additional demand that might be created by the food facility could be expected to have little effect on world price. The effect could be considerably greater when a bad harvest reduces world stocks and a second bad production year forces developing countries to import greater quantities than normal.

It is interesting that prices increased sharply in 1973 when the ratio of stocks to demand dropped from 18.5 to 15.5 percent in one year. The price increase was considerably larger than our estimation, and this indicates that speculative buying and hoarding probably drive prices higher than their equilibrium level because of uncertainty about future market behavior. With the facility in place, some of that uncertainty may be reduced. To the extent that the facility reduces uncertainty about access to supplies by assuring access to cheap credit to finance cereal imports no matter what the price, some of the incentive to corner large supplies in a high-price market may be reduced. Over the longer term, market reactions to the existence of the food financing facility could reduce price shocks, despite the pressure of additional demand. Even a small increase in average grain prices would have some lagged effect on production. Similarly, an increase in price variability would increase the profitability of holding stocks of grain and so increase grain stocks. Thus, the expected responses of production and stocks could offset some of the effect of the food financing facility on the level and variability of international market prices.

Appendix. Methodological Notes

THIS STUDY WAS CONCEIVED by the authors as a follow-up to research on the costs and benefits of an insurance scheme to provide food security for developing countries with food shortages. The objective was to consider the merits and probable effect of alternative schemes that might actually be adopted by an international organization. In addition to drawing on previous work, three new activities were planned.

First, it seemed worthwhile to visit a few representative developing countries to find out how much government officials felt lack of foreign exchange constrained food imports and to obtain their views about the usefulness of a food financing facility. Countries visited included Bangladesh, Egypt, Senegal, Brazil, and Peru. Even though its cereal imports have declined sharply since 1976, India was included as a sixth sample country because of the size of its food requirements and the high probability that a substantial shortfall in domestic production would occasionally necessitate large-scale imports.

The selection of countries was to some extent arbitrary. The countries included, however, represent a diversity of situations with respect to geographical region, population size, income level, degree of self-sufficiency, degree of financial constraint, and variation of domestic policy. Table 12 gives data for the indicators used to show the diversity of the countries chosen.

The brief country visits and interviews were not meant to provide a definitive analysis of the food security position of any

Table 12. *Indicators of Food Import Vulnerability for Six Countries, 1976 to 1978*

Region and country	*Population, 1976–78 (millions of people)*	GNP *per capita, 1976–78 (1977 U.S. dollars)*	*Cereal import volume, 1976–78 (thousands of metric tons)*	*Share of cereal imports in staple consumption, 1976–78 (percent)*	*Share of cereal imports in export earnings, 1976–78[a] (percent)*	*Coefficient of variation for total staple consumption, 1961–77*	*Average per capital calorie intake as percentage of* FAO/WHO *standard 1977–79 (percent)*
Asia							
Bangladesh	77.8	86	1,355	9	12	7.6	77
India	641.3	155	2,852	2	6	5.3	90
Africa							
Egypt	39.4	326	5,079	44	13	12.6	111
Senegal	5.2	365	425	31	13	15.7	94
Latin America							
Brazil	116.2	1,419	3,978	9	4	5.8	105
Peru	16.2	726	1,037	30	7	3.9	90

a. Excluding value of food aid.

Source: Barbara Huddleston, *Closing the Cereals Gap with Trade and Food Aid* (Washington, D.C.: International Food Policy Research Institute forthcoming); and A. Valdés and P. Konandreas, "Assessing Food Insecurity in Developing Countries," in Alberto Valdés, ed., *Food Security for Developing Countries* (Boulder, Col.: Westview Press, 1981), chapter 2.

of the sample countries. Nor was there any attempt to develop a common questionnaire or interview technique. Each author visited the assigned countries to meet and talk informally with individuals in key ministries and public agencies. In general, each sought to determine the degree of commitment by various countries to consumption stabilization policies that could involve considerable fluctuation in the level and cost of cereal imports from one year to another; to discuss with senior officials their perceptions of the usefulness of a food financing facility compared with other food security measures their governments were already pursuing or planning; to learn what specific responses their governments had made to past situations requiring an unusual import response; to ascertain whether these officials considered other problems, such as logistical or managerial constraints, more serious than the availability of foreign exchange; and to verify the production, consumption, and trade data available from official sources.

From these discussions, the authors formed some impressions about the variety of country situations that a financing facility might have to address and the hypotheses most appropriate for testing in the analysis of the potential effect of a food financing facility. Thus, the visits helped in formulating the design of the study and the subsequent analysis reported here.

Second, a simulation model was created to test the effect on food security of a financing facility operating under three different specifications and to compare the results with the situation if there were no facility. The model estimated a country's food consumption based on plausible determining factors, including probability distributions of domestic food production, the price of imported food, and the availability of foreign exchange. Food security with and without a financing facility operating under various rules was simulated on the basis of 3,000 randomly drawn observations from these probability distributions. The experiments were repeated with different sets of parameters reflecting different government policies, and the results were used to assess the effects of alternative financing arrangements.

Finally, it was decided to perform some simulations with price-forming equations for wheat to ascertain the order of magnitude for price changes that could be anticipated from shifts in demand created by a financing facility.

The Simulation Model

This section briefly describes the equations and decision rules of the simulation model used to test the effect on food security of a financial facility under three different specifications and to compare these results with the situation if there was no facility.

The demand for food in any year is

$$C_f = a_0 - a_1 P_f$$

where C_f = food consumption and P_f = price of food.

Initially the model estimates consumption, C_f^c, and price, P_f^c, without imports, that is,

$$C_f^c = Q_f$$

where Q_f = domestic food production. Solving these two equations yields the closed economy price of food

$$P_f^c = a_0/a_1 - (1/a_1)\ C_f^c.$$

Next it is determined whether and how much imports are desired:

$$I_f^* = \begin{cases} 0 & \text{if } P_f^c \leq P_f^i \\ C_f^* - Q_f & \text{if } P_f^c > P_f^i \end{cases}$$

and, if desired imports are positive, desired consumption is

$$C_f^* = a_0 - a_1\ P_f^i$$

where P^i is the import price, and I_f^* and C_f^* are the desired amounts of imports and consumption. Whether these or different amounts are actually obtained depends on the amount of foreign exchange allocated to food imports. How the model handles the foreign exchange constraint is discussed in a subsequent section.

The desired levels of imports and consumption are not necessarily determined by private demand. The government can decide to import more or less than what consumers are willing to buy at the prevailing border price, or, alternatively, it can tax or subsidize imports. In the policy stipulated to analyze the effectiveness of different financial facilities, the government intervenes to make the domestic prices more stable than the world price. This is equivalent to imposing a more inelastic demand through subsidizing imports when the world price is high and taxing imports when world price is low.

Figure 17 illustrates the difference between the two policies. *DD* represents private market demand, and *dd* represents the demand with government intervention. If in a given year production is Q_f, there is a positive demand for imports ($P_f^i < P_f^c$). Desired consumption is C_f^{*u} without government intervention and C_f^{*s} with government intervention. Similarly, the respective desired import levels are $C_f^{*u} - Q_f$ and $C_f^{*s} - Q_f$. The corresponding domestic prices are P_f^i and P_f^s. If in another year production, Q_f, is between Q_f^{*u} and C_f^{*s}, there would be no imports if the government does not intervene to stabilize consumption, whereas with intervention a positive import demand exists.

To analyze whether desired imports will be actually obtained, foreign exchange becomes constraining when

$$M_f^* + M_{nf}^* > X$$

where M_f^* and M_{nf}^* are the desired amount of foreign exchange for food and nonfood imports, respectively, (at the prevailing exchange rate), and X is total foreign exchange availability. Under a completely flexible rate of exchange regime and without

Figure 17. *Consumption with and without Government Intervention to Stabilize Price and Consumption*

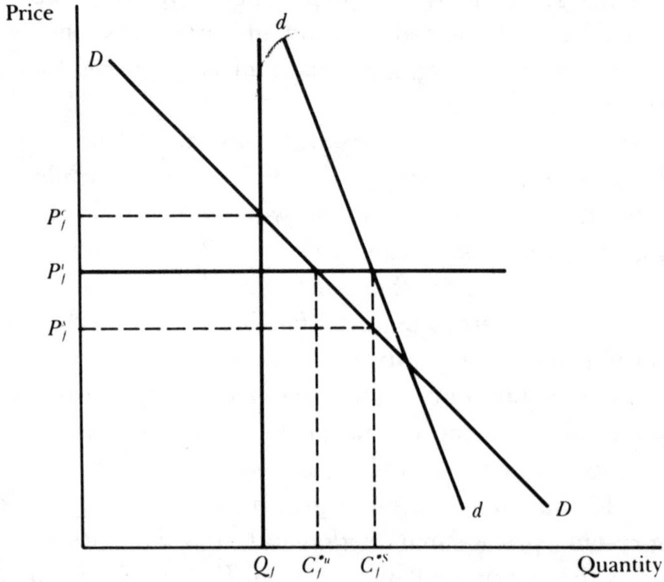

import controls, an excess demand would bring about a change in the exchange rate and proportional reductions in the desired demand for both food and nonfood imports. More realistically, however, allocations of foreign exchange to food and nonfood imports in scarcity situations is often made on the basis of political and other considerations, that is, different implicit exchange rates for food and nonfood imports prevail.

To highlight how different propensities of governments to restrict foreign exchange to food imports (m) will influence the effect of a financial facility on food security, the allocation model is specified as follows

$$M_f^{*'} = \begin{cases} M_f^* & \text{if } M_f^* \leq X_f \\ M_f^* + m\,(X_f - M_f^*) & \text{if } M_f^* > X_f \end{cases}$$

where $X_f = X - M^*_{nf}$. Similarly,

$$I_f = \begin{cases} I^*_f & \text{if } M^*_f \leq X_f \\ I^*_f + m(X_f - M^*_f)/P_f & \text{if } M^*_f > X_f \end{cases}$$

and

$$C_f = \begin{cases} C^*_f & \text{if } M^*_f < X_f \\ C^*_f + m(X_f - M^*_f)/P_f & \text{if } M^*_f > X_f. \end{cases}$$

The government's propensity to restrict foreign exchange for food imports when foreign exchange is scarce, m, can take any value between 0 and 1. A country that accords high priority to food security will give first priority to food imports, that is, $m = 0$, and actual imports will always be desired imports. At the other extreme, $m = 1$ implies that the food import bill will not be allowed to exceed X_f and that food imports will be restricted to X_f/P_f.

The three financial facilities analyzed provide for drawings of foreign exchange as follows:

$$\text{SAFE} = \begin{cases} 0 & \text{if } X \geq \overline{X} \\ (\overline{X} - X) & \text{if } X < \overline{X} \end{cases}$$

$$\text{SFIB} = \begin{cases} 0 & \text{if } M^*_f \leq \overline{M}_f \\ (M^*_f - \overline{M}_f) & \text{if } M^*_f > \overline{M}_f \end{cases}$$

$$\text{INTEG} = \begin{cases} 0 & \text{if } X - M_f^* \leq \overline{X} - \overline{M}_f \\ (\overline{X} - X) + (M_f^* - \overline{M}_f) & \text{if } X - M_f^* > \overline{X} - \overline{M}_f. \end{cases}$$

In summary, whether and to what extent food consumption in a particular year falls below a critical limit depends on (a) domestic production and the world price of food, (b) the availability of foreign exchange, (c) the country's policy for insulating the domestic price from world price fluctuations, (d) the country's propensity to allocate foreign exchange to food and nonfood imports, and (e) the type of financial facility available for reducing the foreign exchange constraint.

Depending on the combination of circumstances, the effect of a financial facility on food security can range from practically zero to very large. The contribution of a financial facility to nonfood imports is inversely related to its effect on food security. The assumptions concerning the propensity for allocating foreign exchange to food and nonfood imports are highly arbitrary. At best, they indicate only generally the range of likely behavior of governments. For simplicity, the model also does not capture changes in real income attributable to changes in the external account.

Data and Parameters Used in Simulation Experiments

The simulated import price of cereals is a skewed distribution with a mean of US$225 per ton, a median of US$205 per ton, and a standard deviation of US$50 per ton. Ninety-five percent of the time, the price is between US$155 and US$345 per ton. The parameters assumed for the level and stability of cereal production, the availability of foreign exchange for cereal imports, cereal consumption, and cereal imports when production

Table 13. *Basic Country Data Used in the Simulation*

Country	Cereal production (millions of tons): Mean	Cereal production (millions of tons): Standard deviation	Foreign exchange available for cereal imports[a] (millions of U.S. dollars): Mean	Foreign exchange available for cereal imports[a] (millions of U.S. dollars): Standard deviation	Cereal consumption at mean import price (millions of tons)	Cereal imports at mean import price (millions of tons)
Bangladesh	19.0	1.4	425	70	21.0	2.0
India	130.0	8.0	400	450	130.0	0.0
Egypt	8.0	0.37	800	200	12.0	4.0
Senegal	0.75	0.19	77	50	1.1	0.35
Brazil	28.0	2.7	660	500	31.0	3.0
Peru	1.5	0.12	250	100	2.6	1.1

a. Assumed to equal the mean value of cereal imports.

Source: FAO data for production, consumption, and imports; IMF data for foreign exchange.

and the food import prices are at their mean values are shown for the six sample countries in Table 13. Private market demand for all countries is assumed to be a linear function of price, with an elasticity of −0.3 at the mean world price and mean country consumption. Stabilized consumption is correspondingly analyzed through a linear demand function with price elasticity of −0.1 at the mean import price and mean consumption.

Changes in the World Price of Wheat Caused by the Facility

The effects of a financial facility on the world price of wheat were determined in two steps. First, two estimates of the additional demand that might be created by a facility were derived: one based on the deviation of actual imports from a five-year moving trend for 1961 to 1968, and the other based on the deviation of actual imports from the level of imports required to maintain per capita cereals consumption at its 1961–65 average level.

Second, a price-forming equation was derived. Following earlier work by Barr, Adams and Behrman, and Konandreas and others, described in Chapter 5, it was assumed that world stock levels and variation in import demand would have an important influence on price variability. Although substantial explanatory power is lost in attempting to capture price behavior through a single equation, it was felt that as long as the equation tracked historical price variation well and coincided with other theoretical work on wheat prices, it could indicate the likely effect of demand changes, such as those resulting from a food facility.

Several specifications for a price-forming equation were investigated, and the conclusions of Barr, and Adams and Behrman that the level of stocks in relation to demand is an important variable in predicting cereal prices proved useful in estimating wheat prices. The relation of stocks and demand to price is expected to be nonlinear and downward sloping so that response of prices to the ratio of stock to demand is greater when the ratio is lower; demand shocks, given high relative stock levels, are thought to have a negligible effect on prices. Drawing further on the work of Adams and Behrman, time trends in price as well as the current period response of prices to expected demand or actual forward contracting were explored.

Using ordinary least squares and the Corchran-Orcutt procedure for correcting for serial correlation, the following price-forming equation was selected to track wheat prices:

$$\ln P_t^w = 9.08 + \underset{(2.16)}{7.17} \ln (ES/D)_t + \underset{(2.48)}{1.55} /(ES/D)_t - \underset{(-2.95)}{0.039}\, T$$

with $\rho = 0.42$, $R^2 = 0.60$, $\overline{R}^2 = 0.62$, $DW = 1.71$, and $F(3, 13) = 9.55$ for 1961 to 1978 where $P_t^w \equiv$ world price of wheat in 1977 U.S. dollars in calendar year t; $ES_t \equiv$ total world cereal ending stocks for the crop year ending in year t; $D_t \equiv$ total world cereal demand for the crop year ending in year t; $T \equiv$ time

Table 14. *Estimated and Actual Wheat Prices Associated with Different Ratios of World Cereal Stocks to World Demand*
(1977 U.S. dollars per ton)

Ratio (percent)	Estimated price[a]			Actual distribution[b]	
	1962	*1970*	*1978*	*Years*	*Price*
14.0	394	288	211		
14.5	346	253	185		
15.0	309	226	166	1975	153
15.5	280	205	150	1973, 1976	219, 135
16.0	257	188	138	1974	228
16.5	239	175	128		
17.0	224	164	120		
17.5	213	156	114	1978	108
18.0	204	149	109		
18.5	197	144	105	1971, 1972, 1977	132, 133, 96
19.0	191	140	102	1966	153
19.5	187	137	100		
20.0	184	134	98		
20.5	181	133	97		
21.0	180	132	96		
21.5	179	131	96	1962	157
22.0	180	132	96	1963, 1967	154, 150
22.5	180	132	97	1965, 1968, 1970	145, 151, 132
23.0	182	133	97	1964	163
23.5	184	135	99		
24.0	186	136	100	1961, 1969	154, 144
24.5	189	139	101		
25.0	193	141	103		
25.5	197	144	105		
26.0	201	147	108		
26.5	206	151	111		

a. Estimated prices are based on the function:

$$\ln P_t^w = 9.08 + 7.17 \ln (ES/D)_t + 1.55/(ES/D)_t - 0.039\ T.$$

Each value of the ratio of stocks to demand yields a corresponding price estimate. Because a time trend element (T) is included, the set of price estimates shifts downward over time. Ratios of stocks to demand are presented with the corresponding price estimates for 1962, 1970, and 1978.

b. Actual prices and the years in which they were observed are tabulated to correspond with observed ratios of stocks to demand.

Source: Estimated prices from IFPRI calculations; actual prices from World Bank data.

(1961) = 1; and figures in parentheses represent the t values. This estimation supports the hypothesis that wheat prices have had a declining secular trend and that the price response to import demand shifts becomes increasingly important as the ratio of stock to demand drops (see Table 14).

Various attempts to constrain the ES/D variable by using a threshold above which an increase in ES/D would yield no marginal increase in ρ were inconclusive. Threshold values were defined alternatively as 0.17, 0.20, and 0.22 percent for ES/D. Several different values were tried for the variable M, but none yielded satisfactory results.

References

Abbott, Philip C. "Modeling International Grain Trade with Government Controlled Markets." *American Journal of Agricultural Economics*, vol. 61 (February 1979), pp. 22–31.

Adams, Gerard F., and Jere R. Behrman. *Econometric Models of World Agricultural Commodity Markets*. Cambridge, Mass.: Ballinger Publishing Company, 1976.

Barr, T. N. "Demand and Price Relationships for the U.S. Wheat Economy." *Wheat Situation*, No. WS225 (August 1973).

Behrman, J. R. *Foreign Trade Regimes and Economic Development: Chile*. Foreign Trade Regimes and Economic Development. Vol. 8. New York: National Bureau of Economic Research, 1976.

Bigman, D., and Shlomo Reutlinger. "Food Price Stabilization: National Buffer Stocks and Trade Policies." *American Journal of Agricultural Economics*, vol. 61, no. 4 (November 1979).

Food and Agriculture Organization of the United Nations and UN World Food Council. "World Food Security: The Need for Balance of Payments Support to Meet Exceptional Variations in Food Import Bills." Rome, January 1980.

Gilmore, Richard, and Barbara Huddleston. "The Food Security Challenge." *Food Policy*, vol. 8, no. 1 (February 1983), pp. 31–46.

Green, Christopher, and Colin Kirkpatrick. "Insecurity, Food Financing and the IMF." *Food Policy*, vol. 6 (August 1981).

Goreux, Louis. *Compensatory Financing Facility*, Pamphlet Series no. 34, Washington, D.C.: International Monetary Fund, 1980.

Huddleston, Barbara. *Closing the Cereals Gap with Trade and Food Aid.* Washington, D.C.: International Food Policy Research Institute. Forthcoming.

International Monetary Fund. "Decision on Compensatory Financing of Fluctuations in the Cost of Cereal Imports and Consequential Amendments." Washington, D.C., May 14, 1981.

Johnson, D. Gale. "The World Food Situation: Developments during the 1970s and Prospects for the 1980s." In *AEI Studies on Contempory Economic Problems.* Washington, D.C.: American Enterprise Institute, 1980.

Konandreas, Panos, Barbara Huddleston, and Virabongsa Ramangkura. *Food Security: An Insurance Approach.* Research Report no. 4. Washington, D.C.: International Food Policy Research Institute, 1978.

Lofchie, M. F. "Agrarian Crisis and Economic Liberalization in Tanzania." *Journal of Modern African Studies,* vol. 16, no. 3 (1978), pp. 451–75.

McIntire, John. *Food Security in the Sahel: Variable Import Levy, Grain Reserves, and Foreign Exchange Assistance.* Research Report no. 26. Washington, D.C.: International Food Policy Research Institute, 1981.

Morrow, Daniel T. *The Economics of the International Stockholding of Wheat.* Research Report no. 18. Washington, D.C.: International Food Policy Research Institute, 1980.

Pitt, M. M. "Alternative Trade Strategies and Employment: Indonesia." In A. O. Krueger, H. B. Lary, T. Monson, and N. Akrasanee, eds., *Trade and Employment in Developing Countries.* Vol. 1. *Individual Studies.* Chicago: University of Chicago Press, 1981.

Reutlinger, Shlomo. "Food Security: Magnitude and Remedies." *World Development,* vol. 6 (1978), pp. 797–811.

———. "Policies for Food Security in Food-Importing Developing Countries." In A. H. Chisholm and R. Tyeis, eds., *Food Security: Theory, Policy, and Perspectives from Asia and the Pacific Rim.* Chapter 2. Lexington, Mass.: D.C. Heath, 1982.

Scobie, Grant M. *Food Subsidies: Their Impact on Foreign Exchange and Trade in Egypt.* Research Report no. 40. Washington, D.C. International Food Policy Research Institute, August 1983.

———. *Government Policy and Food Imports: The Case of Wheat in Egypt.* Research Report no. 29. Washington, D.C.: International Food Policy Research Institute, 1981.

Siamwalla, Ammar, and Alberto Valdés. "Food Insecurity in Developing Countries." *Food Policy,* vol. 5, no. 4 (November 1980).

U.S. Department of Agriculture, Foreign Agricultural Service. *Foreign Agricultural Circular—Grains.* FG-28-81. Washington, D.C., July 1981.

Valdés, Alberto, ed. *Food Security for Developing Countries.* Boulder, Col.: Westview Press, 1981.

Warner, Dennis Lee. "An Econometric Model of the World Wheat Economy." Ph.D. dissertation, Princeton University, Princeton, N.J., 1979.

World Bank. *Commodity Trade and Price Trends.* Washington, D.C., 1979.

Index

The full range of World Bank publications, both free and for sale, is described in the *Catalog of Publications;* the continuing research program is outlined in *Abstracts of Current Studies*. Both booklets are updated annually; the most recent edition of each is available without charge from the Publications Sales Unit, Department B, The World Bank, 1818 H Street, N.W., Washington, D.C. 20433, U.S.A.

Barbara Huddleston is a research fellow and Alberto Valdés is director of the International Trade and Food Security Program at the International Food Policy Research Institute. D. Gale Johnson is Eliakim Hastings Moore Distinguished Service Professor and chairman of the Department of Economics at the University of Chicago. Shlomo Reutlinger is senior economist in the Agriculture and Rural Development Department of the World Bank.